Dear Dorothy,

You are so special to the Lord —— He calls you "PRECIOUS"!

Esther

High Pasture

Surviving the Journey

Esther Walker

RIVERSTONE GROUP
PUBLISHING

ISBN 0-9706117-8-1

Cover design by: Mary Long, Market Connections, Asheville, NC

Interior design by: Riverstone Group, LLC, Canton, GA

Scripture quotations are from the following versions:

Quotations noted as KJV are from The Holy Bible, KIng James Version, KJV. Public domain.

Quotations noted as NKJV are from The New King James Version of the Bible. Copyright © 1979, 1980, 1982, 1982, Thomas Nelson, Inc., Publishers.

Quotations noted as NIV are from The Holy Bible, New International Version, NIV™. Copyright © 1973, 1978, 1984 by New York International Bible Society. Used by permission of Zondervan. All rights reserved.

Quotations noted as NLT are from The Holy Bible, New Living Translation, NLT, Copyright © 1996. Used by permission of Tyndale House Publishers, Inc. Wheaton, IL 60189. All rights reserved.

Quotations noted as Amplified Bible are from The Amplified Bible, Expanded Edition, Copyright © 1987 by The Zondervan Corporation and the Lockman Foundation. All Rights Reserved.

Quotations noted as J. B. Phillips are from The New Testament in Modern English, J. B. Phillips, Copyright © J. B. Phillips 1958,1960, 1972. LETTERS TO YOUNG CHURCHES © Macmillan Publishing, Co., Inc. 1947, 1957. All rights reserved.

dedication

Dedicated to the ones God calls "Precious"—my grandchildren, who are all in the springtime of their journey on their way to High Pasture . . . following the Shepherd.

In order of appearance . . .

Jay

Katie

Erin

Hope

Amy

Adam

Cameron

Ian

Micah

Joshua

Jamie

Jonathan

Emma

acknowledgements

God's timing is perfect....the idea of this story came twelve years ago. Looking back I see the many dear friends who made this book possible—who made the lamb live.

So often I would lay the manuscript down and wonder if it could be of any real value to God's Kingdom. Then someone would come with just the right encouragement and help I needed.

Carol Jackson was the first one God sent. She loved the first few chapters and began typing with great enthusiasm. When we moved away her final words to me in a letter were "do not give up finishing this book."

Lorna Israel, an efficient secretary at the church was eager to help and began typing as the chapters developed.

Then Susan Daigle came into my life with her computer expertise and picked up the story. When she moved away—the lamb was put to bed again.

But when Mary Jones, a gifted secretary, appeared and was willing to spend hours typing and retyping the many pages of the nearly finished manuscript—the lamb began to walk again!

When Susan Daigle moved back into town, she carefully put together all the changes and additions—and the manuscript was almost complete.

Then came Pam Tessier, the talented new secretary, who was to wrap it all up. She made the final changes and additions and with her computer skills and organized mind, she soon had the right publisher and all the minute details worked out!

But there were others . . .

My thanks to my friends Brenda Schuller and Dottie Setran for reading the manuscript and encouraging me along the way.

My thanks to Lance Mericle, our graphic designer, who studied the drawings, made suggestions, contacted the publisher and worked on the cover.

My thanks to Mary Long from Market Connections who designed the final cover, and told me great stories about the wee lamb she raised.

My thanks to Troy Tolle, our talented photographer, who made me really look "good."

My thanks to my children who encouraged and anticipated the completion of the book.

My thanks to my son, James, who got busy and "made things happen" at the finish line.

My thanks to my sweet husband, Ian, who liked the story from the start and kept telling me . . . "finish it."

Thank you,

Thank you,

Thank you.

contents

introduction

The strength and simplicity of the 23rd Psalm has comforted and sustained many broken and wounded people down through the centuries. I, too, have been warmed and encouraged in its sunshine many times.

But, in retrospect, I realize that my ability to appropriate its truth has been very limited. Along with so many others, I really did not understand the tender relationship that exists between the sheep and the shepherd. I could not appreciate the everyday, routine experiences of the flock, which make up such a large and significant part of their lives, nor the crises that come by surprise.

If, for a while, I could leave the busy, complicated environment in which I live, and walk in the small footprints of a lamb as it grows and develops through the seasons of life, I would notice truth I have never seen before. If I could sense the needs of the sheep and feel their emotions, the whole Psalm would take on new meaning.

Spending delightful hours on the path and in the pasture with the flock, walking with them through the changing seasons, I have been refreshed and blessed.

I have been reminded of the frailty and helplessness of the lamb, and I remember that God's power is seen more clearly in my weakness.

I have been reminded of the minute and momentous needs of the sheep, which are never ignored or overlooked by the Shepherd, and I am awed by His tender, loving daily care in my life.

I have been reminded that the sheep's safety in the present and its hope for the future do not depend on its strength, cleverness or strong faith, but on the presence of the Shepherd.

I have been reminded that the Shepherd doesn't cast aside the foolish and failing sheep, but carries them, and I realize that the battle is not mine—but God's.

With overwhelming gratitude, I have been reminded that in God's eyes—I am Precious!

This is an allegory . . . the routine experience of the lambs and the rest of the flock are meant to portray human conduct and experience. So there are hidden spiritual meanings that transcend the literal story. The "Selah" at the end of each chapter is a means of explanation as we "pause and think about it."

JEHOVAH
ROHI
The Lord
Is My Shepherd
Psalm 23:1

"AND THE WHISTLE AND THE THUMP HARMONIZED INTO A SAD LITTLE DUET."

Chapter 1

The small creature stood still for a moment to catch His breath. He had been running wildly from one direction to another, and now he was too tired to lift his feet. His weariness came not only from the frantic physical exertion, but also from the confusion and fear that pumped and twisted through his shivering body.

He was standing now on a bleak and barren plateau. It was a favorite place for the icy wind, for no tree or hill hindered its freedom; it whipped around the shivering form of the little creature as if eager to meet someone in such a lonely spot. As it rushed by, it seemed to whistle in the little one's ears,

"Why-y

ar-re

you-u

he-e-ere?"

The steady thumping of the creature's heart, the only other sound there was, seemed to answer that, and all other questions which might follow,

"I-don't-know.

I-don't-know."

The whistle and the thump harmonized into a sad little duet there on the barren plain. Suddenly, the creature realized that the faint rumble of thunder in the distance was growing louder. The ground beneath his feet trembled at the intrusion of the ominous roll.

The gray clouds plunged and tumbled over the head of the helpless one and he shuddered in fear at the deepening darkness. Oh, how he wished for a place to hide!

Suddenly, almost above his head, a bolt of lightning split the sky and shattered the heavy darkness with an eerie incandescence. In that moment, one electric word crackled through the air . . . LOST!

The immediate thunderclap that followed was, to the little creature, the collision of two giants—"Reality and Truth!" Fright slapped him so hard that, once again he began to run. It is no wonder that in a matter of moments he tumbled pell-mell, head-over-heels, down into a deep and narrow ravine.

There he lay, still as the pile of rocks around him, oblivious to the cruelty of the persistent rain that pelted his fragile frame without mercy.

Finally, the storm had dumped its fury and the thunder slowly receded into the misty distance from which it came. From high above, radiant beams of light swept silently down; the rays diffused and danced through the great, billowing clouds. The storm was over and there was no stopping the sun!

Golden beams easily found their way into the ravine and filtered gently through the eyelids of the little one. He moaned softly, then slowly lifted his head and blinked his eyes, stunned by the sudden splendor of the brightness around him.

Struggling to his feet, still blinking, he looked up at the towering shaft of jagged rock that loomed above his head. He gasped as he looked down, for he was standing on a narrow ledge jutting out above a deep chasm. Fortunately, the little one did not look high enough to see the sharp-eyed vulture circling slowly above him in hungry anticipation.

A dusty, green, speckled lizard poked its head out of a crevice in the cliff, and with bulging half-closed eyes, stared with cold curiosity at the trembling intruder. In his pitiful state, the fallen one was grateful for even this companionship; but the scaly reptile was an unfriendly and pitiless thing which had no inclination to comfort him. The two stood staring at each other for a moment; and then, with two whip-like expulsions of a long, forked tongue, the lizard turned and disappeared into the rocks. High above, two other shadows joined in the sinister circling—their piercing eyes were glued on the white speck on the ledge.

The fallen one felt utterly alone and he shuddered. His head throbbed and a twinge of sharp, hot pain shot through his back and down his right leg. Tiny, red spots had dried and stained the ledge under him, and the scrapes and scratches began to sting. To add to his plight, he realized that he was hungry.

He shivered as shadows gathered around him in cold patches of black and gray. The warmth of the sunshine had been his only source of comfort, and now even that was going. Suddenly, great, black wings slapped the air above him, and he screamed out in terror.

It was not a loud cry, this pathetic, bleating sound that fear had squeezed out of the feeble creature; but it was loud enough to be heard by the keen ears of the One who searched for him.

The voice that fell upon the ears of the little animal was, to be sure, the most welcome, the most thrilling and beautiful sound that he had ever heard.

"Oh, there you are, my foolish lambkin. You have gotten yourself into a fine mess now, haven't you? Do you know that I have searched for you this whole day?" He paused for a moment, then after a weary sigh of relief, He continued, "I'm so glad I heard your cry. Don't be afraid now, little one, I am here."

That voice penetrated the suffocating shadows like a shaft of light and echoed down the dismal canyon like majestic music. Hope surged through the lamb's frail frame, for without a doubt, he recognized that voice . . . that wonderful voice. It gave him strength to look up; and there, leaning over the cliff, gazing down with tender concern, was the face of his hope, his help, his joy . . . The Shepherd!

Without hesitation, The Shepherd began to lower His staff, turning it carefully, until its well-planned curve was firmly positioned under the body of the shivering lamb. Then, with a strong and steady arm, trained by many experiences such as this, slowly, carefully, He began to lift the little, limp body.

Somehow, the lamb sensed that to struggle and resist now would mean his doom, so the helpless one surrendered himself to the strength and wisdom of The Shepherd . . . and the upward pull was glorious!

Soon he found himself in the safe arms of The Shepherd, who placed him gently on a patch of soft, green moss and then sat back to look at him.

As the bruised little one stood on wobbly legs, facing The Shepherd, he lowered his eyes. He had been so foolish and reckless and certainly deserved whatever his punishment might be. A surge of terror shook him so hard that he fell to the ground.

"Steady there, my precious one," The Shepherd said softly, as He held him up with His right hand. With the other hand, He began to pull the briars and twigs from the tangled coat of the shaggy little lamb, brushing away the dry mud from his face.

"Well, you haven't broken any bones, it seems, but you have some pretty deep cuts; they may leave some scars, but you will make it." As He spoke, He pulled a little flask of olive oil from under His leather belt and began to pour it on the wounds of the trembling lamb.

It was then the little lamb noticed for the first time that The Shepherd's hands were bleeding.

" Oh no!" he thought. "It's all my fault. What will He do to me now?"

But to his surprise, when The Shepherd lifted him gently in His strong arms, and pressed him close to His heart, the fear melted away like ice in the summer sun. There in the gathering shadows of evening, high on a dangerous mountain cliff, The Shepherd stood smiling down at a bedraggled little orphan lamb, nestled safely in His arms, fast asleep.

There was no memory of the long and difficult trudge back to the flock; but when the lamb lifted his head, he found himself safe at home in the fold. He stood up slowly on unsteady legs and looked around as though he were seeing it all for the first time. He had never noticed what a beautiful place it was. Now, to be sure, the place had not changed; but indeed he had!

Up to this moment, he had watched The Shepherd from a distance, afraid of one so big and powerful. He had heard the grown-up sheep call him by name, but the lamb had felt too small and insignificant to mention The Shepherd's name out loud . . . but now . . . remembering the comfort of His strong arms and the warmth of His kind words, it was different. The Shepherd had searched for him as though he were His only lamb—as though he were important—as though he were "Precious."

The lamb stood gazing at The Shepherd standing in the midst of His flock, and whispered softly . . . "Emmanuel."

Now, The Shepherd's voice gave the lamb special joy; and when He gathered His sheep around Him and began to speak, Precious understood, for the first time, what He was saying!

"I myself will search and find my sheep. I will be like a shepherd looking for his scattered flock. I will find my sheep and rescue them from all the places to which they were scattered on that dark and cloudy day.

I myself will tend my sheep and cause them to lie down in peace, says the Sovereign Lord. I will search for my lost ones who strayed away, and I will bring them safely home again. I will bind up the injured and strengthen the weak. . . ." (Ezekiel 34:11,12,15,16A—NLT)

Selah

pause and think about it

There are age-old questions—plaintive cries that echo down the crowded corridors of time. They are as old as the human halls in which we walk. "Who am I? Why am I here? Does it even matter?"

It is the eternal quest and query. It is the hunt for some sort of explanation for all of "this." We seem to make an appearance in this world as a creature of chance, to struggle and grow and struggle some more. We try to find a spot of our own, a place where we belong, hoping that in that spot we will be happy.

Happiness ahead becomes that illusive and just-out-of-reach goal. We chase after it, and if for a moment we catch it, like a gossamer bubble, reflecting a rainbow, it bursts, leaving only a wet spot in our hand.

It is easy to see why we find ourselves running wildly in all directions just like the little lamb. There are some animals that can survive in the wilderness when left to themselves—but not sheep; they are helpless creatures, frail and often foolish.

A little lamb lost in the wilderness would be in a pitiful plight, for it would soon be eliminated by the elements or devoured by the wild animals that seem to thrive in desolate places.

Lost is a cold and lonely word, and we shiver in fear at the sound of it. We are sent running to escape its insidious implications. Since the terrain of everyday living is sometimes steep and treacherous and we are not prepared for mountain climbing, it is not surprising that we find ourselves bruised and bewildered on some rocky ledge of trouble and perplexity.

However, that hard place, although narrow and uncomfortable, is the best spot to land, for it forces us to stop and evaluate our unsafe and serious condition. It is not until we "come to an end of ourselves," and are unable to get anywhere anymore, that we look up and cry out to God for help.

Oh, the power of that upward look and cry! To our amazement, we discover that He is really there! His name is "Emmanuel"—God is with us down here! And if we trust ourselves to His strong arm, He will reach down to lift us up. God, Himself, bends down to pull us up when we have hit the bottom! He is the only One who can remove the briars of guilt and the mud of our mistakes. He is the only One who can heal the cuts and scratches of injured relationships and broken dreams. He is the only One who can soothe the open, draining sore of a broken heart and even make something beautiful and worthwhile out of smashed things.

God, Himself, picks us up and holds us close to His heart—from the hole to His heart! What an amazing thought. Our position is completely and eternally different. We are safe in His care, no longer lost and alone, wandering in the desert of defeat and despair.

God, Himself, calls me "Precious," no longer a mere creature at the mercy of the weather. I am His Darling, I am His—and He is mine!

"Oh, wondrous thought—how can it be
that such a One considered me?
Across wild plain and mountain steep,
My Shepherd searched for me—His sheep.
He heard my cry from high above,
and now I'm safe—lifted by love!
Oh, wondrous truth, oh joy sublime,
for I am His—and He is mine!"

"What do you think? If a man owns a hundred sheep, and one of them wanders away, will he not leave the ninety-nine on the hills and go to look for the one that wandered off? And if he finds it, I tell you the truth, he is happier about one sheep than about the ninety-nine that did not wander off. In the same way, your Father in heaven is not willing that any of these little ones should be lost." (Matthew 18:12-14–NIV)

JEHOVAH
JIREH
The God Who Sees and Provides
Genesis 22:14
"I Shall Not Want"

Chapter 2

"Faithful" was a gentle, old ewe that had quietly followed The Shepherd for many years, and everyone saw the strong bond of love between them. She had mothered many lambs, which lambs now had lambs of their own. Precious began to notice that the small Faithful ewe had to walk more slowly now, and The Shepherd took great care not to walk too rapidly ahead of her.

But, today, Faithful wasn't walking at all; and Emmanuel sat in the shade of an old oak tree, holding her tired head in His hands. Precious thought that this must be one of the times to be sad because everyone said that she was dying, and that sounded sad to him. But as the lambkin stood quietly at The Shepherd's elbow, mustering all the sadness he had, he found it to be quite difficult. The air was fragrant with a special kind of quiet joy, and a hint of lovely anticipation of something wonderful about to happen.

Every now and then, The Shepherd leaned down and whispered into old Faithful's ear, and she would smile ever so faintly. Precious tried his best to get close enough to hear, but he soon realized that this marvelous moment was meant for only the two of them. However, because he pressed so close, Precious saw something he had never seen before. There, glistening silently like tiny diamonds, were tears in Emmanuel's eyes. They stayed there even as he smiled down at His beloved sheep.

Since this was a purely private moment, Precious moved back and turned his attention to the thick patches of sweet, red clover, sprinkled luxuriously over the meadow, glancing now and then at The Shepherd, of course.

Before he knew it, he had backed into something; he turned around quickly, nearly poking his nose through a rusty, wire fence.

"Whoops!" he sputtered, jumping back. (Glancing, of course, at The Shepherd, still sitting under the tree.) There, on the other side of the fence, stood a scrawny lamb about the age of Precious, curiously watching Precious nibbling and glancing.

"Hello," said Precious, "what's your name?"

"Oh," she said, "I'm Hungry."

"Me, too," replied Precious as he bent down for another bite.

"No, I mean, that's my name—Hungry," said the scrawny one.

"That's a peculiar name," Precious replied, without even missing a nibble.

"The hireling says it suits me," she continued, "and he's right for once, 'cause I'm always hungry. You sure are lucky to live on that side of the great, wide fence."

"No, I'm not," Precious responded quickly, realizing something for the first time; "I'm not lucky—I'm loved! The Shepherd knows the best pasture and I just follow Him. I belong to Him, you know."

He was looking proudly at Emmanuel as he spoke now, and the words seemed sweeter than the nectar in the clover.

"Well, call it what you will," said Hungry, "but just be glad you are not on this side of the fence."

For the first time, Precious realized that the clover banquet stopped at the fence! All the "hungrys" on the other side had nibbled and chewed every green thing that could be found. Except for a few lonely tufts of grass here and there, the dry earth lay exposed looking embarrassed and sad, pounded down by many anxious hooves.

"Is that who owns you . . . the hireling?" asked Precious.

"No," Hungry answered, "he's just hired to tend us. Ha! Some tending he does! I have never met the one who owns us, and I don't think I want to."

The sad, little lamb paused just a moment, deep in thought, and then continued sadly, "Anyway, I know he doesn't care anything about me. I just try to keep out of the hireling's way. I'm looking and hoping to find something good to eat and some nice, coo-ool water." She tilted her head slightly and closed her eyes as though she was about to taste it; then she sighed and said, "You see, I'm thirsty all the time, too."

Precious hadn't taken a bite for a while now because he was tasting sadness. "Yes," he thought, "this is a time to be sad for the little thirsty lamb on the other side." He would have liked to share his meadow with all the hungrys, but they could not get through that tall, rusty fence.

By this time, Hungry had turned to continue her search for something succulent and didn't pay any more attention to Precious, who stood with his nose sticking through the fence gazing sadly at the thin, little lamb slowly wandering away.

"I'll go tell Emmanuel," thought Precious. "He has plenty of love to go around."

He turned and ran as fast as he could, straight to The Shepherd, who was gently carrying the very still form of an old, satisfied sheep.

Realizing that this was not a time for words, Precious walked quietly behind Him, so grateful to belong to One so kind and loving. As he walked, he whispered softly,

"Thank you. Thank you.

Thank you. Thank you.

Thank you. Thank you."

The big flock kept The Shepherd very busy. Precious thought that surely their constant needs, some big and urgent, some small and silly, would tire Emmanuel so much that He might finally hire someone to help Him care for them. Hearing of the reputation of the hireling, Precious didn't want Him to do that, so he decided to keep his concerns to himself; but the haunting face of "Hungry," now sketched indelibly upon his mind, never left him. He really missed "Faithful," too, and often he stood quite still gazing into the distance, wondering exactly where she went, why she had to go, and would he have to leave the flock one day, too?

In the days that followed, Precious did not realize that something strange was happening. Small lumps began to appear on his back and slowly grew larger and larger; gradually they began to affect him. He couldn't seem to keep up with the grasshoppers in the tall grass anymore because there was no "ump" in his jump. He was also losing the desire to chase the butterflies fluttering playfully above his head. Yes, the growing lumps on his back were getting larger and heavier, and they were, most definitely, slowing him down.

One day, as he stood thoughtfully by a still pool of water, he glanced down and saw his reflection gazing up at him. He was (of all things) frowning! Indeed, there on his fleecy forehead was a furrow for sure.

He jumped when a gruff voice behind him asked, "Whatcha' lookin' at Lumpy?"

"My name is not Lumpy," Precious said as he turned to face a big ram standing behind him. "It's Precious. P . . . r . . . e . . . , well anyway, my name is Precious."

"Oh, is it now?" the ram said, with a twinkle in his eye. "How come? You look like a 'Lumpy' to me."

o o o o THANK YOU o o o THANK YOU o o o THANK YOU o o o THANK YOU o o o

Precious tried to look back over his shoulder at his reflection in the pond, but he couldn't see over the lumps; so he turned around slowly and then looked down into the water again. The ram was right! He did look like a "Lumpy!"

"Oh no!" thought Precious, "I've lost my name too!" He began to cry, and he couldn't seem to stop.

The big ram moved close behind the sobbing little lamb and spoke more gently.

"I didn't mean to make you cry, son. We all get lumpy now and then."

That welcome thought; and the confident voice, seemed to comfort Precious a little bit, and his sobbing slowed down to a loud sniffle and a snuff.

"That's better, although a good cry now and then is good for a case of the lumps," the big ram said smiling.

"Why?" asked Precious, drying his tears on one of the soft pendent leaves of the willow tree that leaned over the pond.

"Because the tears wash your eyes so that you can see the lumps, of course! Once you see them, you will know what to do with them."

It was true, because Precious could see better now, and he recognized the face of the big ram. He was one of the respected leader rams of the flock, and his name was "Steadfast". Everyone warmly called him "Old Steady."

"Hey," Steady continued, "aren't you that little guy that used to stick so close to The Shepherd? We used to say, "Now there's a smart little lamb. Emmanuel will be able to make something of that one!" Then he added quickly, "What are you doing here, son?"

The tears had done their best, because Precious saw something very clearly. He saw that he could not see The Shepherd! The troubled lamb had slowly wandered off; thought after thought, worry after worry, sigh after sigh, until The Shepherd was out of sight.

"Oh, no!" cried Precious, looking wildly about, "gotta go!"

He began to run as rapidly as his legs and lumps would allow him (which was not very fast.) When he finally reached the top of the hill, he was really out of breath, but that didn't matter, for at that ponderous moment, he wanted to find The Shepherd more than anything else in the whole world. Suddenly, a big smile burst on his face, so big that the impact pushed

the frown right off his head, because there, on the other side of the hill in the middle of the 21peaceful flock, stood his Friend—The Shepherd.

In his eagerness to get back to The Shepherd, he nearly tumbled down the hill because the lumps threw him quite off balance. He waddled and limped as quickly and carefully as he could among the sheep grazing peacefully around The Shepherd. At last, in sweet relief, he threw himself down at His feet.

"Ah, there you are, my Precious one, I've been missing you. My, my, what a load you are carrying. Come close and I will lift them off your back."

There, on the windy meadow, on The Shepherd's lap (lumps and all), Precious began to tell Him all about his meeting with "Hungry." The tears ran down the face of the little lamb as he described his skinny, new friend. He told The Shepherd about his own terrible fear of the hireling and how he shuddered to think that person might one day be hired to look after him. He told Him how much he missed Faithful and his confusion about where she had gone so unexpectedly. He told The Shepherd that he was afraid that maybe one day he, too, would have to leave the flock and go somewhere, perhaps far away. On and on he went, while Emmanuel listened, quietly holding the little bothered one in His arms. One by one, the tenacious tufts of worry and fear loosened and fell at the feet of The Shepherd. Precious glanced down and saw the pitiful things lying there, unattached and harmless; he was so relieved that he wanted to jump down, and run and kick up his heels in the cool grass.

However, the wise Shepherd kept His arm around the eager little lamb and said quietly, "Wait, little one, don't run away so quickly. You have told me all, now you must take time to listen. You have given me all your cares, now I want to give you something. You see, I don't want you to miss anything this morning."

Emmanuel's gentle words made Precious hesitate. He looked up lovingly into The Shepherd's face, so close to his, and nearly burst out into laughter at the foolish thought of leaving that wonderful spot on His lap so soon! The Shepherd's presence was far sweeter than the honey in the sweetest, red clover; more beautiful than the whole spring meadow; and far more refreshing than the freshest mountain stream. The little lamb's eyes filled with clear, warm tears of joy as he pressed close to Emmanuel.

As Precious sat still and listened, his Shepherd began to speak softly about the clumsy burdens that lay scattered at His feet.

"Give all your worries and cares to me, for I care about what happens to you."(I Peter 5:7—NLT)

Now, Precious really did not want to discuss those burdens or even look at them again, so he decided to keep his eyes closed and just lean and listen.

The Shepherd continued, "I'm so pleased that you have met little "Hungry" and are concerned about her. We shall plan together how to help her; you see, I love her, too! Precious opened his eyes quickly, at the sound of these welcome words.

"Oh, I'm so thankful!" he whispered happily.

Then The Shepherd said, "The hireling you fear shall never own you, my lamb. You are mine and no one can pluck you out of my hands."

"Whew! I'm so relieved," breathed Precious as The Shepherd continued.

"My ewe, Faithful, whom you miss so much is just fine; far better than ever she was. She is in a pasture so gloriously beautiful, that it cannot be described to your little ears."

"Yippee," shouted Precious, "I'm so glad!"

"I know that you miss her very much," He spoke softly, "and the loneliness hurts. But if you could see what I see, you would joyfully agree to the pain; and you would approve and admire the reason for it . . . for there is a reason."

The little lamb was quiet for he knew that he had been given a truth so deep and wonderful that it would take a very, very long time to understand it, but he began to try.

"Here is something else for you to think about," The Shepherd said, smiling. "One of these days you will see Faithful again and she will be strong and beautiful and radiant with joy—not old and weak!"

"Oh, wonderful!" shouted Precious, as he leaped from The Shepherd's lap.

Suddenly, he paused and stood looking down at one of the lumps lying at The Shepherd's feet and said thoughtfully, "But, I will have to leave my lovely pasture that I know so well, to see Faithful. How will I get there? And when . . . and . . ." As he spoke, he was unconsciously leaning over to pick up some limp lumps that had been removed from his back.

"Wait, my impatient one, you are off my lap now," The Shepherd said firmly.

Precious dropped the burdens he was picking up, as if they were hot, and climbed quickly onto his Friend's lap without saying a word.

"Do you know that I love you, Precious?" Emmanuel's voice was soft and serious now.

"Oh, yes! I know you love me," Precious answered quickly. "Each time I see the deep scars in your hands, I am reminded of your love for me."

"Then," replied The Shepherd, "will you trust me with your future?"

The little lamb was silent now. His future was the biggest and most important thing he had! But, he realized that his answer would reveal the condition and size of his love for Emmanuel.

He looked toward the misty blue mountains in the distance and thought:

I trusted Him to rescue me
From the hole in which I had rolled,
I trusted Him to carry me
To the shelter of the fold.

I trusted Him to hold me close
And provide refuge from the cold.
I trusted Him to hear my sighs,
Dry my tears and lift my load.

Surely—One so great and loving
My tomorrows can safely hold,
In His hands my pathway glistens,
Paved with promises of gold!

And the grateful little lamb cried, "Yes! Oh yes! I will trust you with my future. You are the only one who knows what to do with it! Of course, I want you to have it! If you are my Shepherd I shall never be in want; for you see what I really need and you provide for me. Yes, yes, yes . . . yes . . . yes!"

The evening breeze picked up the sweet affirmation and mixed it with the fragrance of the Evening Primrose just opening its silken petals to welcome the sunset . . . the heart of the rescued lamb was also opening to welcome a new understanding of Emmanuel's love.

Selah

pause and think about it

Fences are an important part of the landscape of this world. From the sharp, barbed wire of the prison to the ivy-covered wall of the palace, they stand as silent sentries guarding man-made boundaries.

A fence may be high or low—rock, wood, or wire—depending on its purpose; whether it is intended to be a protection or a confinement, a boundary or a barrier.

At times, a shepherd will use an enclosure or sheep-cote to protect his flock against the night predators that would prey on them, or the thieves that would steal them away.

But most of the time, the sheep are out in the field with their shepherd. He owns them . . . they belong to him, and he has a deep, personal interest in each one. The sheep sense his love and have discovered, through the many experiences of danger and hardship, that he can be trusted. This trust produces obedience, and as they listen to his voice and follow him, they are able to enjoy a "fenceless freedom!"

This is not so with the sheep that belong to the hireling, for he tends to them out of cold necessity instead of warm concern. They do not know him or trust his meager provision and careless protection. These insecure and dissatisfied sheep definitely need a fence, or they will surely wander off. Jesus said:

> *"I am the Good Shepherd. The Good Shepherd lays down his life for the sheep. A hired hand will run when he sees a wolf coming. He will leave the sheep because they aren't his and he isn't their shepherd. And so the wolf attacks them and scatters the flock. The hired hand runs away because he is merely hired and has no real concern for the sheep. I am the good shepherd. I know my own sheep, and they know me." (John 10:11-14—NLT)*

How wonderful it is to be on the right side of the fence! To belong to Jesus, the True Shepherd and Guardian, to recognize Him as my owner means that I have escaped the confinement behind the barbed wire of hopelessness.

It is a fact the sheep out in the field are in imminent danger of wild animals and thieves. But if they were to concentrate on these chilling circumstances, they would live in a constant state of restlessness and panic, and certainly could not enjoy anything.

No, this peace in the pasture comes from the simple, uncomplicated dependence upon their strong shepherd who watches over them. Although we do not credit sheep with great intelligence, they seem to be way ahead of us in the trust department!

I must admit that many of my precious moments have been wasted in the restless and unnecessary confusion of worry. In the midst of spiritual plenty, I have spent hours in impoverished foreboding and dark imaginings, somehow forgetting that God, the Holy Watcher, sees what is going on and knows what to do about it.

When the storms of life hit and the solid ground of our faith gets muddy and slippery, it is easy to slide into the soggy furrow of forgetfulness.

When we begin to concentrate on the mud instead of the Master . . . we forget about His wisdom and beauty.

When we begin to concentrate on the lightning instead of the Lord . . . we forget about His power and strength.

When we begin to concentrate on the thunder instead of His voice . . . we forget that He is speaking to us.

Care, like gravity, pulls our attention down and we become earth-bound. The "realness" of God recedes into the distance and burdens are allowed to pile up, one on top of the other. Left to ourselves, it is possible to remain in this uncomfortable and heavy condition for a long time, and finally accept the load as our lot in life. But, just as the lamb is fortunate to be part of the flock, so we are fortunate to be part of the family of God, the Church!

God knew, from the beginning of time, that we would need each other. When overcome and ready to collapse in despair, the "overcomers" who have been where we are, and have felt what we feel; and have come out on the other side, are able to comfort and encourage us.

"All praise to the God and Father of our Lord Jesus Christ. He is the source of every mercy and the God who comforts us. He comforts us in all our troubles so that we can comfort others. When others are troubled, we will be able to give them the same comfort God has given us" (2 Corinthians 1:3-4—NLT)

When we are weak and unsteady in our faith, the steadfast ones are strong enough to lift our attention from the "earthly" to the Eternal, and direct us into the Throne Room! The wonderful invitation has been sent to us, and the door is wide open!

"So let us come boldly to the throne of our gracious God. There we will receive His mercy, and we will find grace to help us when we need it." (Hebrews 4:16—NLT)

Oh, what we miss outside the Throne Room! A century ago, Joseph Scriven wrote these wise words that have become more beautiful as the years go by:

What a friend we have in Jesus, all our sins and griefs to bear!
What a privilege to carry everything to God in prayer!
Oh, what peace we often forfeit, oh, what needless pain we bear,
All because we do not carry everything to God in prayer!
Have we trials and temptations? Is there trouble anywhere?
We should never be discouraged, take it to the Lord in prayer.
Can we find a friend so faithful who will all our sorrows share?
Jesus knows our every weakness, take it to the Lord in prayer.
Are we weak and heavy laden, cumbered with a load of care?
Precious Savior, still our refuge; take it to the Lord in prayer.
Do thy friends despise, forsake thee? Take it to the Lord in prayer;
In His arms He'll take and shield thee; thou will find a solace there.

God wastes nothing. He is able to take the burdens that weigh us down and make good use of them. Anything that throws us into the arms of the Good Shepherd is worth it!

God even uses our tears, whether they flow from grief or relief. The dust and pollutants around us cloud our vision, and the tears wash our eyes so that we are able to see what is really important and what is not.

The songwriter, David, declared joyfully:

You will show me the path of life;
in Your presence is fullness of joy;
at your right hand there are pleasures forevermore.
(Psalm 16:11–Amplified Bible)

But what an enigma! We are told that God will fill us with joy if we spend time in prayer, and the pleasure that we find in His presence will last forever. Yet, we so often rush into His presence, climb upon His lap and present our long list of needs—then we jump down and run on our way—in too much of a hurry to listen and enjoy our dearest Friend!

Hurry, flurry, and *worry* are words that rhyme, and rightly so, because they go together.

Duty calls and cares beckon,
"Come away for it is getting late.
Hurry now, this is very important!"
But the Father whispers . . . "wait."
"Stay, little one, stay with Me,
you will miss Peace if you pull away.
The longer you stay in My arms, My love,
The stronger you will meet your day!"

Sheep learn by experience that their shepherd can be trusted. They are either too naive or too smart to be concerned about the future. The shepherd is there and that seems to be all that matters to them. To us that sounds far too simple to be wise.

We may trust Him in the present sunlit moments that are in our sight—ah, but the future, with the possibility of mountains higher than we have ever climbed, with earthquakes very high on the Richter scale . . . that is another matter.

We seem to stand on the mountain of the moment looking into the heavy fog that completely obliterates our view . . . wondering what is out there.

What a relief to discover that our Great Shepherd, our Emmanuel, knows what is in the dense fog of tomorrow . . . He has already been there!

JEHOVAH
The Lord is my Peace
Judges 6:24
SHALOM
He maketh me to lie down in green
pastures. He leadeth me beside
the still waters

Chapter 3

Precious was wide awake very early the next morning. He watched the golden rays of the sun hug the mountains and then lean down and awaken his meadow. He was standing knee-deep in cool, green grass. Tiny, diamond drops glistened on each blade. The dew hung daringly on the tips of the green leaves of the tall lilac bush, heavy and fragrant with lavender blossoms.

Precious moved under the bush with his face turned upward and his mouth open wide as he saw the dew slipping off the leaves; he laughed out loud when it splattered playfully on his nose instead.

How Precious loved the early moments of the day! It seemed as though he was seeing the world just newly born into creation. He gazed up into the regal lilac bush towering over him. Crowded clusters of lavender blossoms swayed quietly over his head. The beautiful sight nearly took his breath away, and he wondered how such beauty could be so quiet. Surely this magnificence should be accompanied by some sound to attract the attention of the sleepy world.

The lamb was right, for as he stood gazing he heard a faint whisper as the awakening wind touched the blossoms. Yes! There were words and music to the beauty.

The greatest Truth is born in silence,
And the sweetest song is sung at dawn.
These can't be heard in loud defiance
But patiently wait till the noise is gone.

Precious tried to hold his breath so that he could hear it all. "Oh," he thought, "to think I almost missed the music! I'm glad I stood still long enough to hear it!" And he ran to tell Emmanuel what he had heard.

Each day, Precious discovered something new in the meadow.

He had grown to love the familiar beauty all around him and thought that it would always be the same. One day he began searching for the tall bush loaded down with lilacs; he wandered around and around the spot where he was sure it stood, but he could not see one solitary blossom, only thick, green heart-shaped leaves.

He had spent hours looking for the sunny, yellow forsythia that glowed all over the hillside, but they were gone; only graceful, green bushes swayed in the wind. And to top it all, his favorite, blue hyacinths had disappeared! How he longed for their sweet perfume, but it was gone. Everything seemed to be changing. It made him sad, and even a bit scared.

The disposition of the once peaceful flock was changing too. It was growing more and more restless and irritable as the days grew warmer and the grass became dry and sparse. Each seemed so touchy now, and Precious had learned the hard way not to bump into the old ewes while they were eating. More than once, without a warning of any kind, an old ewe would lower her irritated head in anger and butt him, sending him sprawling.

Not only had summer taken over the meadow, but a great buzzing army of insects had taken over, too. Precious thought about telling The Shepherd about the difficulty he was having with them, but, they seemed so small and insignificant, surely he could handle them by himself.

So, when they tickled his nose, he shook his head very hard and they flew off . . . for a moment. He was quite proud that he could defend himself so well. When they stung his ears, he rubbed his head against the rough shoulder of a tall rock and the pests flew off . . . for a moment; but then they were back again, buzzing and biting and tickling. He had shaken his head so long, that he was getting a bit dizzy; and he had rubbed the rocks so hard, that his head hurt. So he decided the only thing left to do was to run and hide from his enemies. He now spent most of his sunny days running from one hiding place to another, but they followed him relentlessly. While standing in a shady thicket, tired and nervous, feeling very sorry for himself, and wishing he had something good to eat, he thought he heard someone calling his name. He stopped shaking his head just a minute.

Yes, there it was again! "Precious, where are you, my lamb? Precious." A great wave of cool relief swept over him as he recognized that voice. He forgot all about the flies and burst out of the thicket shouting, "Here! Here I am Emmanuel, here I am!"

In a few moments, his Friend was kneeling at his side. Precious was so tired and relieved that he collapsed on His lap with a whimper and a sigh. Instantly aware of the bothered lamb's predicament, The Shepherd reached for His oil and with expert hands began to soothe the irritated little head, gently rubbing the ointment on his ears, around his eyes and even on his nose. It didn't smell good and he wanted to protest; but in a moment, he realized that the flies didn't like it either, and they were gone! Aahh—sweet, sweet relief, and he leaned back and rested in his perfect hiding place, The Shepherd's lap.

"You will feel better now, my little one." He said smiling, as He patted the weary lamb.

"They were so little . . ." Precious moaned softly, trying to explain his predicament.

The Shepherd smiled sympathetically, and said, "They fooled you, didn't they? You have discovered how even small things can cause big trouble. You must learn to come to me with even your little annoyances; remember, I love you and I know how to handle every nuisance."

Precious felt rather ashamed that he would have to be reminded of the truth he had learned before. But, there was no anger or harshness in The Shepherd's voice and so he joyfully relaxed in His presence.

In a few moments he was on his feet again looking for something to eat! "Oh yes," The Shepherd said, laughing, obviously enjoying the lamb's speedy recovery from misery, "I was looking for you to tell you that we are all moving on to summer pasture today. I know of greener pastures higher up the mountain. Come little one."

The thought of leaving his familiar pasture frightened him, but he knew that wherever his Shepherd would lead him would be the best place to be. So, he skipped willingly behind The Shepherd as they passed the tall, rusty fence.

"The fence!" gasped Precious. "Oh, I must find Hungry."

He ran along beside the tall fence calling as loud as he could, "Hungry, Hungry! Where are you?"

There was no answer, so he kept running and calling. Suddenly he saw a tall, scrawny ram, busily gnawing some roots near a pile of rocks on the other side of the fence. Small clods of mud were perched on his nose, and dried clumps clung to his shaggy coat under his chin.

"Have you seen my friend, Hungry?" asked Precious, breathlessly.

The ram looked up, noticeably irritated at the interruption of his meager meal.

"Whatcha want her for? She ain't worth nothin'. She's sick," he said gruffly, as muddy juice dripped from the side of his mouth.

"Sick!" cried Precious. "Where is she?"

"She and her maw, and a bunch of other strays are bein' loaded into a truck jest about now," the ram muttered, squinting his eyes as if studying the sun, still munching his muddy roots.

"But where are they going?" Precious asked anxiously.

"Where do you think, stupid . . . to the market!" the ram shouted.

Precious was so afraid of the rough ram that he was shaking. He tried to steady his voice as he asked one last question. "P-P-Please, sir, what is the m-market?"

The ram burst into loud laughter, mud flying in all directions. It was a relief to see him laugh, even though it didn't make him look any more pleasant.

"That's the end of the road, boy! Fin-ished! Kaput! The owner . . ." He hesitated for a moment and Precious could see terror in his eyes as he lowered his head and his voice and continued:

"The owner is taking them . . . to be slaughtered."

"Slaughtered!"

Precious didn't need that word explained. He could tell that it meant something terrible, so he turned and ran as fast as he could to tell The Shepherd.

He was out of breath when he finally stood beside his Friend, who listened attentively while the gasping little lamb explained what he had heard.

"Please, please, save Hungry and her mother. I don't want to move to higher ground without them!" And he buried his face in The Shepherd's sleeve and sobbed.

Precious could not even imagine what could be done to help them, for it looked so impossible and it seemed too late. But, as he gazed into the face of Emmanuel, so strong and wise, hope, like a tiny candle, flickered in the troubled gloom.

The Shepherd rose to His feet and steadied Precious on the ground; his eyes were very serious now. He reached down and patted the lamb confidently; then after giving some brief orders to two of His dependable rams, Steadfast and Unity, he turned His face toward the village.

Under the watchful eyes of Steady and Unity, the flock gathered together in the sheepfold. Precious watched his tall Shepherd stride up the hill and disappear into the distance.

The flock stood quietly in the fold, speaking softly to each other, apparently aware of The Shepherd's mission. But, Precious began pacing back and forth. Every few moments he stopped and stretched his neck, straining his eyes to see over the sheep and into the gathering darkness. The old familiar frown was back on his fleecy forehead.

Hours passed and there was no sign of The Shepherd. The pacing was making his legs weak, the stretching and straining made his neck and eyes hurt, and the frowning was giving him a headache. He was beginning to think that loving someone caused too much pain and he wondered if it was worth it. If he had never met Hungry, he would have probably been sound asleep now—and The Shepherd would not have been caused all this trouble.

Suddenly he stopped short and shook his head violently, ashamed and surprised at his selfish thoughts. All of his worrying and weariness, his fearing and nervousness was making him reason foolishly, he thought; but this didn't give him any comfort.

Just then he looked up into the face of a beautiful Ewe who had been watching him as he struggled with his dilemma. She was smiling down at him and he was grateful to have his thoughts interrupted by such a lovely face.

"Let's sing!" she said pleasantly. "SING!" Precious nearly gasped! What a ridiculous thing to say at such an obviously worrying moment. Then he recognized the pretty ewe named Psalm. She was always singing some new song she had learned about Emmanuel. Precious looked into her face and decided quickly that her peaceful eyes surely had never seen trouble.

"No wonder she sings all the time," he thought. "I can't expect her to understand what I'm suffering now."

Frowning politely, he said, "I know you mean well, ma'am; but, I don't feel like singing. I'm scared, and the least I can do right now is worry!"

"Ah," she said, with a sigh, "I see that you have met "the Stalker."

Precious glanced over his shoulder, expecting to see someone, but there was no stranger in sight. A bit bewildered, he asked, "Who is 'the Stalker'? and where is he?"

"He is a thief, lamb, and he is not far away. The Shepherd calls him "Fear." He is always following the flock waiting for an opportunity to steal our peace."

Just then Precious realized that she was right . . . HIS PEACE WAS GONE!

Seeing the frightened expression on the face of the lamb, she added quickly, "Don't pay any attention to him, lamb . . . just resist him the moment he comes around and TRUST THE SHEPHERD–HE CHASES HIM!"

It was that word "trust" that jolted his memory, and he remembered The Shepherd's question: "Will you trust me with your future?" Precious had promised to trust Him with his future; but, it was Hungry's future he was worried about now. Then, like the rays of sunlight at dawn, a wonderful truth shined in upon his troubled heart–because of his love for Hungry, his own future was strangely entwined with his little friend. . . . Hungry was part of his future!

"Do you know any songs?" Psalm asked, interrupting his thoughts once again.

He replied slowly, "Yes . . . I know a song, but it is very hard to sing in the dark, isn't it?"

"Yes, little lamb, it is," Psalm agreed. "But try."

And so hesitantly Precious began to sing his old song . . . very softly, of course:

I trusted Him to rescue me
From the hole in which I rolled.
I trusted Him to carry me
Into the shelter of the fold.

To his surprise he found that it felt good to sing in the dark, so he sang a bit louder, as brand new words slipped out of the shadows:

I can trust Him with my loved one,
For He wants me to be bold
With confidence I'll wait for Him
To save my friend before she's sold!

"Confidence!" repeated Psalm proudly, "That's exactly what we need!" And she began to sing her own confident song:

Sing praises to God and to His Name!
Sing loud praises to Him who rides the clouds.
His name is the Lord-
Rejoice in His presence!
Father to the fatherless,
defender of widows-
This is God, whose dwelling is holy.
God places the lonely in families;
He sets the prisoners free
and gives them joy.
But for rebels, there is only famine
and distress.

Praise the Lord; Praise God our Saviour!
For each day He carries us in His arms.
Our God is a God who saves!
The sovereign Lord rescues us from death.
(Psalm 68:4-6, 19,20—NLT)

Her song was so beautiful that it wasn't long before Precious had learned the words.

As the two sang together, Precious began to notice that as long as he sang, he didn't worry! Praise, Worry, and Fear could not be companions!

At first, he decided that the songs had some magical power to chase the peace thief and make him feel better; but, the longer he sang the more clearly he saw that it wasn't the song that helped; really, but the theme of his song, who at that dark moment could not be seen—The Shepherd. Yes! He chased the Stalker. . . . He was the source of the singing! Praise was the soul's laughter in the night!

Grateful to discover this new truth, Precious looked up wide-eyed into the face of the gentle ewe, and asked softly, "Where did you learn the secret of the song?"

Psalm seemed to have anticipated the question, because she answered quickly, "The songs came naturally, little one. They are just the sounds of adoring gratitude as my heart overflows with love for our Shepherd. My first song began the cold night He redeemed me from the butcher's block in the slaughter house."

Precious stood still in startled silence for a few moments—realizing for the first time that real trusting is always accompanied by praise and that the greater the gratitude, the sweeter the song!

Suddenly, Steady shouted, "He's coming, The Shepherd is coming!"

Since it was not quite dawn, it was difficult to see through the dim veil of shadows. Not until their Shepherd was very near did they see the straggly band of ransomed sheep walking slowly behind The Shepherd, who was carrying a skinny, sleeping lamb named "Hungry" in His arms.

They had to move very slowly the next day because of the ransomed ones, but nobody minded. The wonderful anticipation of greener pastures seemed to give even the weakest sheep new strength. "Hungry" was far too weak to walk, so The Shepherd carried her in His arms. Precious walked proudly behind The Shepherd, looking after the thin smiling mother of the sick lamb, and whispering softly as he walked,

Thank you,

thank you,

thank you,

thank you . . .

By mid-morning, Precious was wishing that there were an easier way to get to higher ground, for the way was growing steep and treacherous. The Shepherd kept a watchful eye on the obedient flock following Him. Every once in a while He reached down and patted the fleecy head of Precious, as he walked close to The Shepherd's heels. The lamb soon realized that the five little pats had words—"I - am - lov - ing - you." And he smiled proudly.

By noon the air was so heavy with heat that Precious forgot all about smiling. The sun was directly overhead and showed no mercy in its steady glare. He was finding it hard to walk, for even the stones along the way were hot. He was dropping farther and farther behind, and was too tired to care if the other sheep passed him by. He began looking for a shady spot now, a place to stop—for he had taken his eyes off The Shepherd.

In the distance, out of the way, he saw a cluster of tall, gray rocks. Surely he could find a cool shadow there. No one noticed that he left the flock, for each one concentrated on his own weariness.

Sure enough, there between two boulders was a spot of shade neatly guarded by the leaning rocks. It was just his size, so Precious slipped in and stretched out. Ah, how good it felt to stop. He looked up at the stern, silent boulders and smiled in gratitude for their cool provision.

His muscles were aching and his eyelids were heavy, so he rested his head on the cool dirt and closed his eyes. He was almost asleep when he heard the song. The hot wind had lifted it above the shuffling footsteps of the sheep and now carried it on waves of heat, around the rocks, past the drooping ears of the little lamb.

He opened one eye just wide enough to see Psalm. Her head was hanging low, and she walked slowly . . . but, she was singing.

Go quietly on when the way is steep,
Keep your eye on The Shepherd ahead.
Don't forget, He loves each one of His sheep,
And has traveled this path we now tread.

Go quietly on when the ground is hot,
From the searing rays of earth's sorrow
Remember, He is everything you are not,
And He knows what you need tomorrow.

Go quietly on when it takes too long,
And duty stretches to unfair length.
Keep close to your Shepherd, where you belong
FOR THE JOY OF THE LORD IS YOUR STRENGTH.

Precious knew that she had seen him and the song was for him. The gentle words seemed to echo around and over the gray rocks . . . "the joy of The Lord is your strength . . . the joy of The Lord is your strength . . . the joy of The Lord is your strength."

Gradually they drifted off into the dusty distance and were gone, and all he could hear was the lazy buzz of a bee examining the barren boulders above him.

But the song had already done its work; arousing his groggy memory, he slowly raised his head. Suddenly, he could see the reason for his weakness. He had taken his eyes off The Shepherd! Yes, it was the clear sight of Him that had given strength before, and that is why he had none now!

In embarrassed determination, he crawled out from between the boulders and looked up at them. They seemed to glare down at him with a hard, uncaring grin. He had run to the "rock tombs" for comfort! The fright of his foolishness sent him running toward the flock, which was by now, quite a distance away.

He tried calling to them, but they just kept walking. His legs were becoming so weak that he finally stumbled and rolled over on the ground. He lay there with his nose in the dirt; each puff of breath sent a tiny cloud of dust swirling over his head, and his tears made little mud spots on the hot ground.

He was too weak now to cry out, so he just lay there, hot and helpless. It was not until a cool canopy of shade fell upon him that he stirred. He opened his eyes just a bit and looked up into Emmanuel's face. He wanted to cry out in joy, but he only managed a pitiful moan.

When The Shepherd picked him up, ever so gently, and placed him beside Hungry, who was still asleep in His arms, Precious knew that his moan was understood just fine.

Even though the sun beat down upon them as they climbed, and the way was even more steep, Precious didn't mind, for he was above it all in his Friend's strong arms, grateful even for the helplessness that had swept him so close to his Shepherd's heart.

By afternoon they had reached the first ridge of their mountain and The Shepherd stopped. The weary sheep looked up in surprise as a cool breeze caressed their hot faces. They eagerly gathered around The Shepherd as He stood gazing at the green, velvet carpet rolled out before them. Like a silver ribbon, a quiet stream wound its way through the hills.

In the distance, they could see a wide river resting at the foot of the mountains. The refreshing sight gave the flock new energy and it wasn't long before they stood beside the still, cool stream eagerly satisfying their thirst.

Refreshed, the two little lambs ran into the meadow, knee-deep in silky, green grass. Tall yellow-faced daisies nodded their heads in the summer wind, as if to welcome the weary travelers.

Forgetting all about their weakness, Precious and Hungry ran through the meadow discovering patch after patch of sweet, red clover! While the flock pushed their faces deep into the lush provision, The Shepherd moved slowly among them, examining them one at a time.

He carefully removed the sticky briars and twigs picked up along the way, and soothed their cuts and scratches with his oil and they began to relax. The wind whispered gently in their ears as they ate, but not one of them bothered to look up.

Finally, Precious and Hungry had eaten as much as they could hold, so they laid down. The cool earth beneath the grass made a soft pillow for the two little shaggy heads. They stretched out and yawned a bit, enjoying this delightfully satisfying moment. Precious lay very still with his nose between the green blades; through half-opened eyes, he watched a spotted ladybug inch her way up a slender stalk over his head. She didn't seem to mind sharing her meadow with these new arrivals, so the lambs closed their satisfied eyes and fell asleep.

It was quite dark when the sleepers awakened; now a great, white moon smiled down at them. They realized that a few other sheep were beginning to stir also, for Emmanuel was slowly moving among them, gently calling them by name. He beckoned to the two groggy lambs and whispered softly as He walked by.

"Ho, everyone that thirsteth, come to the waters." (Isaiah 55:1–KJV)

Precious, suddenly realizing how thirsty he was, said to Hungry, "It seems that Emmanuel knows our needs before we do!"

They both jumped up so quickly, they nearly tripped Steady as he walked by. "Oops!" he said, "Sorry lambs, I'm not quite awake yet. Are you ready for a drink of delicious distillation?"

"A drink of what?" Hungry asked, in surprise.

"Dew, lambs, dew! It is almost dew-point!" Seeing the lambs' baffled expression, Steady explained: "The Shepherd knows the moment when the temperature is ju-uus-sst right. Soon every leaf and wisp of grass will sparkle with it . . . clear, still water!" And then he added, with a twinkle in his eye, "We can eat and drink at the same time!"

Precious stood wide-eyed at the wonderful thought, and then looked around at all the sheep who were still sound asleep. "But, what about them?" he said. "They didn't even pay attention when The Shepherd called them."

Steady frowned, shook his head, and said sadly, "They will miss it, and they won't even know what they missed. You see lambs, not everybody responds when The Shepherd calls."

They stepped carefully around the sleeping sheep and joined the eager ones who gathered around The Shepherd. Psalm was there and wide-awake, of course, for her best songs were composed at dewfall. They stood watching expectantly for the special moment. A holy hush hovered over the mountain, and the meadow seemed to hold her breath, as if anticipating something wonderful!

Then suddenly, without a sound of introduction, tiny, diamond drops of dew appeared everywhere. Each common leaf, petal, and blade on tree, bush, and ground gathered with uncommon beauty! Even the delicate spider's web, invisible among the bushes, now hung like a queen's jeweled necklace on display.

It was a splendid, silent invitation to come and enjoy the abundant provision, so the sheep pushed their faces deep into the succulent pasture. Precious and Hungry made sure that their nibbling took place as close to The Shepherd as possible. They loved the sound of His laughter when they lifted their wet faces to Him, smiling in loving gratitude.

By the time dawn's first orange tint peeked over the shoulder of the mountain, the sheep had eaten plenty and really wanted to rest. One by one they gathered around The Shepherd, who was sitting under a tall almond tree, quietly enjoying the joy of His flock.

Precious moved close and stood looking at Him in tender adoration. Psalm was lying now at His feet, Steady was at his right hand, Unity at His left. Hungry snuggled up as close to His side as she could. The Shepherd reached out and cupped Hungry's wet chin in His hands and said with a chuckle, "You certainly don't look like a 'Hungry' anymore, little girl. It's time you had a new name."

He paused for a few moments and then continued, "I shall call you . . . *Satisfied*. How does that sound?"

The little lamb with the brand new name sat up straight, her face beaming. She whispered lovingly to The Shepherd, "Oh . . . it is the most beautiful name I have ever had! Can I keep it?"

The Shepherd was silent for a moment and then spoke in a tenderly serious voice, "That, my little one, is up to you. I will never take it from you, it is my gift to you; but, you must be careful not to lose it."

Determined to guard her gift, never to become "a hungry" again, she snuggled up close to her Shepherd and drifted off to sleep . . . looking particularly Satisfied.

Precious climbed up on The Shepherd's lap, secure and content. He too fell fast asleep as dawn's concert of color introduced a new day, and another truth about Emmanuel's love.

Selah

pause and think about it

In the springtime of our lives we spend our moments in the newness of the present tense, and hardly realize that our "now" is changing. We are unaware of the sure and steady movement of the little hand of the clock—and it really doesn't matter to us. We give no thought to what was or is to come . . . this is childhood.

Somewhere in the passage of years, we begin to pick up "things"—responsibilities and problems; they come together in various sizes and shapes. We often rush to God for help to deal with the "big" things. . . . Oh, but those "little" things . . . the skinned knees and paper cuts, the tangled hangers and knotted shoelaces, the flat tires and dented fenders, the mosquito bites and dandruff, the stuck zippers and leaky faucets, the hurt feelings and forgotten appointments . . . the list goes on and on. These are the rascals that ambush and frazzle us.

God's grace REALLY IS AMAZING! Out of all the billions of people in this world, He notices ME! Not only does He notice, but He cares about every detail of my life and is ready and able to supply all the help I need. We have this amazing promise:

"And my God will liberally supply (fill to the full) your every need according to His riches in Glory in Christ Jesus." (Philippians 4:19—Amplified Bible)

"According to His riches!" That means that it is not just a little help from His vast supply—but in proportion to His riches in Glory—His limitless, super-abundance—WOW!

There is certainly nothing wrong with God's ability to SUPPLY the resources we need—but, there seems to be something wrong with our ability to APPLY His resource to our need to put our knowledge of the truth to practical use.

At this moment, I am at the seaside with my family. My husband just came limping in from a barefoot adventure with our grandchildren. There, deeply embedded in the sole of his left foot was a tiny splinter . . . so little . . . so irritating.

I squeezed with my fingers and then probed with a needle as gently as I could, while he sat quietly making strange faces. It would not budge, but hid there intent, it seemed, on using up my precious moments.

Suddenly it dawned on me that THIS was one of those ridiculous "littles" about which I had been writing! It had been such a small and insignificant bit of something, lying there in the sand, ready for some foot to tramp on—now here it was, causing a strong man to limp!

"Hey, wait a minute," I thought, "God cares about our splinters!" "Help me get this thing out, Father," I said. And he did. That little problem was more than a splinter at that moment;

it was a reminder and an illustration of the intense interest and amazing attention of God toward us!

We have all had days when one thing after another seemed to go wrong—something broke, or we couldn't find it, or we ran out of it, or it got in our way. It was almost like a well-planned conspiracy to keep us from reaching our goal.

Years ago I read, or heard someone say, "the same sun that melts wax, hardens clay." It all depends upon the type of material the sun hits. If I am yielded material in the hand of God, He can transform my interruptions into intermissions; where we pause and look up, instead of down. God gets an opportunity to reveal His DETAILED GRACE to my upturned face!

But, He tells us to ASK for what we need—for the "bigs" and the "littles." Those closest to Jesus, the Disciples, had the wondrous privilege of talking to Him face-to-face, even looking into His Eternal eyes. They could actually hear Him laugh and listen to His wise and wonderful words. They could even touch Him, whenever they wanted! But even they had to be reminded that they did not have what they needed because they did not ask for it. He lovingly supplied their needs, all the way from the big wild storm at sea to the little fish breakfast on the shore.

We certainly can't do anything about what happened to us in the past—all the "littles" and "bigs" that made us what we are today. But we can do something about how we react to them now.

With the full width of God's love stretched out on Calvary and the throbbing thoughts of His magnificent mind, pulsating with Power, printed out before us—God has plowed a way through all the muck and mess, the garbage and the gore of this world, so that we can receive His help when we need it . . . Amazing Grace!

We don't need to come into His presence with a whimper and a whine, a wish and a hope! He calls us up out of our pathetic timidity.

> *"Let us then fearlessly and confidently and boldly draw near to the throne of Grace (the throne of God's unmerited favor to us sinners) that we may receive mercy (for our failures) and find Grace to help in good times for every need (appropriate help and well-timed help, coming just when we need it). (Hebrews 4:16–Amplified Bible)*

God does not give us a prayer formula that we can use to get Him to give us what we want, but He invites us to join forces with Him, and agree with Him to defeat the enemy and accomplish what *He* wants. When as little children, needing Daddy's help, we cry out to Him, simply expecting His help—He begins a process of answering. The timing of that process is

His to do with as He pleases. There are always a bundle of lessons wrapped up in the waiting, and when we look back on our lives we realize that His delays were not denials. He was in the process of training us to LEAN on Him—this is called FAITH.

Just look at what God tells us to do with that FAITH:

"But let all those who take refuge and put their trust in You REJOICE; let them ever sing and shout for joy, because You make a covering over them and defend them; let those also who love Your name be joyful in You and be in high spirits." (Psalm 5:11–Amplified Bible)

"Rejoice in the Lord, O You (uncompromisingly) righteous (you upright in right standing with God); for PRAISE is becoming and appropriate for those who are upright in heart. (Psalm 33:1–Amplified Bible)

The only way that I can prove to myself and others, to heaven's watchers and to the devil's crowd, that I am trusting God—IS TO PRAISE HIM. Praise and trust work together to make something beautiful out of something that is not. They are the warp and woof of the woven fabric that God is in the process of designing to clothe us in His majesty!

Praise does not come naturally in our "dark places." To the untrained eye, it may seem like a cruel, cosmic joke to tell us to rejoice when everything is falling apart and we hurt badly. We just don't FEEL like it then. But praise is not a feeling—it is an act of the will—simple, child-like OBEDIENCE to God's orders.

When we praise the Lord, we join in the conversation of Heaven, for it is the heavenly language. When we praise the Lord, we join the sublime choir of the saints and angels around the throne—it's His music. I want to learn the words to the music when I am here below, so that I won't miss a beat when I am swept into Glory!

A few years ago, my husband and I were in a near fatal automobile accident. We were traveling in a small car and were hit broadside (on my side) by a Lincoln Continental traveling at 90 miles per hour! Later we learned that the driver was on drugs and was being chased by the police. Miraculously, Ian, my husband, escaped with no broken bones, just very painful bruises. I was more seriously injured.

Lying in the Emergency Room of a little hospital in Clinton, North Carolina, in the middle of the night, I drifted in and out of consciousness. It seemed that the room was shrouded in a heavy mist and I could not sense the presence of God. I felt that a strange party or celebration was going on somewhere below me, and if I could lift my head and look under the examination table, I would see it.

I kept thinking, "I don't understand. . . . I don't understand. I dwell in the secret place of The Most High. How did this happen? Where are You Lord? . . . I asked for Your protection. . . . I don't understand."

From somewhere in my misty mind, I heard these words: "Where in my Word did I tell you that you would understand?"

I tried to think of a verse that would help me, but only one part of a verse stepped out of the fog . . . "the just shall live by faith . . . the just shall live by faith . . . the just shall live by faith."

I thought, "Then, am I supposed to praise You Lord? Is that right?"

The answer came back quickly—"Yes." Whether it was out loud or only in my thoughts, I don't know, but I began to say something like this:

"Oh Lord, this hurts so bad—I don't understand what's happening, but I will praise You because I know You love me and You can use this awful mess for something good . . . Hallelujah! I praise You Jesus. . . . I praise You, Jesus."

The pain did not go away. . . . BUT THE PARTY DID!

I see now that in that struggling moment, I was giving up my right to understand. Emmanuel was there, and He understood–that was all that mattered. I belonged to Him and this was His problem, these were His broken bones.

God was showing me, first hand, that praise, when offered as a sacrifice has a potent power to prevent defeat on the battlefields of our lives. When we accept His Will and relinquish our right to understand, the power of praise surges through the darkness, turns on the light—and breaks up the devil's party! God was teaching me a very important lesson–one that would last the rest of my life . . . the power of praise!

It is difficult to believe that we could ever forget these dramatic lessons, but we do sometimes. The dust of daily duties can silently cover the shiny truths, and once again God seems unattached and far away. We may find ourselves looking for help from something or someone instead of The Lord . . . forgetting "Emmanuel"–that God is there with us!

Through many bumps and bruises, a toddler learns that cement is hard, and it hurts when he falls down. It's a great moment when the little one discovers that it is smart to listen to daddy and hold on to his hand!

When I take my eyes off The Lord, even for a short time, life gets too hard for me. It has taken me a long time to learn that when Jesus said, "Apart from Me ye can do nothing," He meant apart from Him I can do nothing! Pulled away from Him, I can do nothing; my joy goes, my peace goes, my direction goes, and I can't accomplish anything really worthwhile.

I may appear to be doing "something," but like a poor little gerbil running as fast as he can on a spinning wheel, I am getting nowhere fast. I end up worn out, hot, and thirsty.

Way back in the Old Testament, Jesus cried out:

"Ho, everyone that thirsteth, come ye to the waters, and he who has no money, come ye buy and eat." (Isaiah 55:1–KJV)

Centuries later, when He walked on the dirt of this world, He shouted to the parched crowd around Him:

"If any man thirst, let him come unto Me and drink. He that believeth on me, as the scriptures hath said, out of his belly shall flow rivers of living water." (John 7:37, 38–KJV)

Finally, as The Risen and Glorified King of Kings, He continues to send out this wonderful invitation:

"And The Spirit and The Bride say; Come, and let him that is athirst come. And whosoever will let him take of the water of life 'freely'." (Rev. 22:17–KJV)

Without water, this planet could not exist; it would dry up and blow away. Since Creation, there has been a constant movement of moisture by evaporation, as the sun draws water from the earth and then stores it in the atmosphere as clouds. Trillions of tons of water are suspended in minute droplets that condense and fall upon us as rain. When, for some reason, that cycle is interrupted and the rain doesn't come—there is drought—and we get desperate.

Jesus is that Living Water, and apart from Him, there is a terrible spiritual drought in our lives. No wonder in that dry desert of despair people do desperate and disastrous things!

Not only does God give us refreshing rain, but He also gives us another beautiful supply—a quiet provision, hardly noticed or appreciated by most of us . . . THE DEW. After a warm day, the moisture condenses and appears silently during the night in tiny crystal droplets. The time of the evening when this begins is called "dew-fall," and the temperature at which the dew appears is called "dew-point." The dew arrives only in the stillness of the night and disappears in the heat of morning sun.

God provides an extra watering for us—a "Dewing" for our souls:

There is a special dew-point in the night
When heat and fury of the day is through;
Where earth is given chance to regain might,
And bathe itself in pure resplendent dew.
So when my life grows hot and worn with care.
My Father calls me to a quiet place.
His Presence cools my heart from earth's bright glare,
So that dawn reflects His Grace in my face.

Before dawn . . . before our eyes look at our responsibilities and chores lined up in a row . . . before there are human footprints on the surface of our soul, we can be "dewed." Alone with our Father, who is waiting to meet with us, our restless racing minds can be steadied and our thoughts organized. Our tense muscles can be soothed and our throbbing hearts strengthened by the peace of His presence.

In that special dewy stillness, God has us all to Himself. Cradled in His arms, we are able to sense our Father's reassuring touch—those five special pats—"I - am - lov - ing - you."

Oh, how sad—too often, we are just too groggy to respond to His invitation, and we sleep on. God isn't disgusted with us, nor loves us less—but WE HAVE MISSED IT! We have missed something wonderful.

JEHOVAH
ROPHE
The Lord Who Healeth
Exodus 15:26
"He Restoreth
My Soul"

Chapter 4

All morning Precious and Satisfied explored their new meadow. They played "hide-and-seek" in the thick bushes, chased butterflies, teased the honeybees, and jumped with the crickets in the tall weeds. Now, they stood at the foot of a grassy hill.

"Wanna race?" Satisfied shouted as she started up the hill.

"No fair! You got a head start," cried Precious as he raced behind her.

They were both out of breath when they reached the top of the hill and lay panting in the cool breeze. In a little while, they sat up and looked down the smooth slope of the other side of the hill. It looked so soft and inviting that they decided to see what it felt like to roll down.

It wasn't long before they were tumbling head-over-heels. It didn't feel quite as good as they expected and both tried to change their mind, but they only tumbled faster! With a thud they hit the bottom and lay there for a few moments, hanging onto the ground as the trees above them moved around and around.

Suddenly, a shrill voice above them shouted, "Willy! Where have you been all morning?" Standing over Precious was a fat ewe (also going around). Precious blinked and sat up dizzily.

"Oh! Goodness. You're not Willy," she said, looking into Precious' face. "Do you know where he is?"

"No ma'am," Precious replied, trying to stand up.

The mother ewe turned quickly and walked off muttering, "That willful lamb will be the death of me."

Satisfied was sitting quietly concentrating on the briers and milkweed pods that had stuck to her on the way down. She looked up and said very seriously, "Let's not do that anymore, OK?"

"OK," replied Precious, still trying to stand up.

Just then there was a burst of laughter from behind a thicket of blackberry bushes. Three plump lambs staggered out. One of them mimicked, "I'm dizzy, let's not do that anymore, OK?"

The other two shouted, "OK, Dizzy!"

Precious and Satisfied stared at them in surprise as the three laughed and staggered around them. Before long they were all laughing!

"I'm Willy," said the first plump lamb, trying to catch his breath. "These are my cousins, Stubby and Luke," he said, tossing his head in their direction.

"I think your mother was looking for you, Willy," Precious replied seriously.

"Why do ya think we were hiding, Dizzy!" Willy exclaimed, and the three burst into laughter again.

"She's always looking for him!" Stubby replied, still laughing.

"Yeah, we spend a lot of time in the blackberry bushes," Luke added, and they laughed louder than ever!

Precious and Satisfied weren't exactly sure what was so funny, but they laughed with them anyway. In fact, they spent most of the day laughing at their new friends. They became completely captivated by their clever impudence, and followed the three pranksters wherever they went.

By evening, they were exhausted and wished that they hadn't wandered so far away from The Shepherd, but it seemed worth it for they had never had so much fun! They wondered why they had not met the three before—perhaps they had stayed too close to The Shepherd and had missed all the interesting sheep who lived on "the fringe" of the flock.

The next few days were filled with excitement and adventure. They climbed and slid on the big rocks at the edge of the river, they scrambled up a steep cliff to eat berries, and even discovered a great hidden waterfall.

Every once in a while, Precious would climb to the top of the green hill to make sure that he could still see The Shepherd. Memories of "dew-point" beckoned to him, but the squeals of laughter behind him held him fast.

One morning while they were hunting for crab apples, Satisfied came running to tell them that she had heard The Shepherd calling their names!

"Oh, dear," said Precious, "I wonder what He wants."

Willy, Stubby, and Luke were quite sure that it was nothing important and encouraged them to pretend they didn't hear. But finally, the three agreed to accompany Precious and Satisfied, at least part way, to see why He had called them. Steady saw the five lambs coming and met them as they approached the flock.

"Well now, here you are lambs! I see you have met Willful, Stubborn, and Lukewarm; no wonder you took such a long time to answer The Shepherd's call," he said, shaking his head.

Precious and Satisfied looked down at the ground a bit embarrassed, as Steady continued. "We must cross the river now lambs, and it is very, very important that we do exactly as The Shepherd tells us, for there is a strong, swift current."

All the sheep gathered around The Shepherd as He spoke seriously.

"Fear not, for I have redeemed you—ransomed you by paying a price instead of leaving you captives. I have called you by your name, you are mine. When you pass through the waters, I will be with you, and through the rivers they shall not overwhelm you."
(Isaiah 43: 1,2–Amplified Bible)

"The sheep that are my own hear and are listening to my voice; and I know them, and they follow me!"
(John 10:27–Amplified Bible)

As The Shepherd began to walk toward the river, Unity moved quickly among the other sheep cautioning them to be very sure to follow very closely behind The Shepherd, for He alone knew the ford, where the river was shallow enough to cross safely.

As the sheep began to move cautiously toward the water, a sly smile crept upon Willy's face and he whispered out of the corner of his mouth, "Hey, I know an even better place than this. C'mon, follow me and we'll beat 'em all across."

Precious and Satisfied both frowned and shook their heads vigorously from side to side, remembering what Steadfast had said; however, the more the three lambs coaxed, the more exciting it sounded to Precious. Finally, he turned and ran off with them, leaving a very worried Satisfied behind.

The four lambs skipped, laughing and shouting along the grass toward the great pile of rocks that had been their playground during the past week. The sandy river bank looked firm and flat as it stretched peacefully out into the water.

"Look, you can even see the bottom!" cried Willy, as he waded out in to the water. Precious was a few feet behind him, just a little bit more cautious. Stubby and Luke stood eagerly on the rocks about to follow.

Suddenly the sand beneath Willy's feet began to shift, and then gave way! Willy struggled frantically for a footing, but down he went under the water! He came up gasping and sputtering; and while the others screamed in terror, the willful lamb was swept downstream, absolutely helpless.

Precious, standing still in the shallow water, tried to turn around and run back, but to his horror found his feet stuck fast in the black, sticky mud beneath the sand. He struggled, but only sank deeper.

Terrified, Stubby and Luke scrambled across the rocks to get away from the river, but their feet slipped off the rocks and jammed down between the sharp boulders. They cried out in pain, but the rocks held them fast.

For a few frantic moments, they screamed as loud as they could, but soon their pitiful cries turned into hopeless little sobs . . . and finally exhausted silence.

The Shepherd had just guided the last ewe and her lamb up out of the water on the other side of the river, and now stood very still studying the surface of the water. His sharp eyes had caught sight of a little white speck bobbing up and down in the water, and His keen ears heard the desperate bleating.

Without a moment's hesitation, he kicked off His shoes and plunged into the river; His strong arms cut through the water with swift, powerful strokes as he swam toward the frantic lamb. But suddenly, while still a distance away, Willy disappeared beneath the water.

In an instant, The Shepherd dove beneath the surface . . . and the river was strangely still . . . not a ripple. Then, suddenly, The Shepherd's face appeared. On His shoulder hung Willy, limp and lifeless.

The Shepherd swam quickly to the shore, laid him on the grass and began to squeeze the still, little form. Leaning down, He began to breath into his nostrils the breath of life. One . . . two . . . three . . . four—no sign of movement, five . . . six . . . seven, and then a slight quiver and a cough—and a breath.

Not far away, Precious struggled for each breath in the choking grasp of the oozing sand and mud, the lightest movement pulled him deeper.

High above his head his old enemies, the black, sharp-eyed vultures began to circle lower, closer and closer. They observed the plight of the helpless creature about to disappear beneath the water, and then turned their attention to the more accessible prisoners, Stubby and Luke, who screamed in terror each time the circling, black shadows touched them! The two little lambs, held in the vice grip of the sharp rocks, were now easy prey to the ruthless predators.

However, the hungry vultures did not know that their ominous presence, while terrifying to the lambs, revealed to The Shepherd the exact location of His fallen ones.

By the time The Shepherd reached the brow of the green hill, two vultures were perched on the rocks close to the trapped lambs . . . waiting. With a loud cry He charged toward them, swinging His rod in circles over His head as He ran. Suddenly, the rod whistled through the air and then, like a mighty fist, slammed into the bird nearest the sheep.

With a startled shriek, and an explosion of wings, the other bird shot up into the air, angry and disappointed. But at the sight of The Shepherd, it rose higher, joining the others, and disappeared in the blue sky above.

Quickly, The Shepherd shifted the sharp rocks that imprisoned Stubby and Luke. Their legs were cut and bleeding, but they were free. Placing them gently on the grassy bank, He rushed to Precious. By this time the lamb was up to his neck in the mire, his eyes were closed, and his breath came in short, painful gasps.

Kneeling down on the bank, The Shepherd pushed the crook of His staff deep into the mud under the lamb. With a strong, steady pull He slowly, carefully drew the limp little body out of the miserable mire.

When Precious opened His eyes he was lying on the cool grass. Emmanuel was leaning over him, gently wiping the mud from his face. The little lamb took a deep, deep breath of fresh air in magnificent relief.

Suddenly the reality of the dreadful, past moments swept over him and he cried out in terror. It was then that his wild eyes met the eyes of his Shepherd. It was this sight that released a torrent of grateful tears that swept away the muddy fear, for he was looking into the face of Love.

"Oh, how can He love me still? What a problem I am to Him," thought Precious. "Oh, how I have failed Him!"

His muddy, little body began to shake with sobs as he thought of Willy and the others, for he was sure they had perished. Oh, if only he could go back and live the last few hours again! Why had he been so foolish?

If only,

if only,

if only,

if only . . .

But, like a great iron door, the past had slammed tightly shut and could never be opened again.

Precious' heart began to pound when The Shepherd picked him up and walked toward the river. Even when he felt himself being lowered into the water that had almost been his grave, he did not resist; for he trusted the strong hands. Once, twice, three times, over and over The Shepherd dipped the lamb. Finally, all the black filth was swept away in the clear water, and once again the little lamb's wool was white as snow.

The Shepherd wrapped the quivering little one in His own shirt and held him securely against His heart. In that warmth the shivering subsided and the rescued lamb was still—he was safe. Great waves of loving gratitude swept over the rescued lamb again and again as The Shepherd walked toward the flock. But, the quivering lamb would never fully fathom the depth of joy in The Shepherd's heart, as He held His Precious one in His arms.

Precious was in for a happy surprise on the other side of the river. The Shepherd made His way through the waiting flock and gently placed him on the soft grass beside his bedraggled companions, Willy, Luke, and Stubby. At the moment, they were a pitiful bunch and they lay very still, lifting their heads just a bit every once in a while to whimper softly.

Precious did not have the strength to get excited at the sight of them. He rested quietly with his nose buried in the sweet grass, watching his Rescuer gently wrap Luke and Stubby's injured limbs. Every now and then, The Shepherd spoke softly to Willy, patting his head (with those five special pats) as He worked.

All that night The Shepherd hovered over His rescued ones as they slept. He knew that fear and guilt had cut more deeply into their souls than any sharp rock could have cut their bodies.

His strong arms had rescued them, His steady hands had tended them, and now His loving presence would comfort and restore them.

Selah

pause and think about it

In the very beginning the man, Adam, lived in the resplendent majesty of God's wondrous presence, and bore the image of his Creator. Since God did not want a coerced love and obedience, He gave to Adam the potentially dangerous power of choice.

At first their fellowship was sweet and pure, unspoiled and unhindered by anyone or anything—beauty and peace reigned in the garden. But, this was just the first phase in God's inexplicably wondrous plan for His precious human race. We read:

The Lord God said, "It is not good for the man to be alone. I will make a helper suitable for him."
(Genesis 2:18—NIV)

So then came Eve—a beautiful companion, just perfect for Adam. She was designed to be a helper and a blessing. But, we discover, to our sorrow, that one day she allowed herself to be influenced by God's subtle enemy, Satan. She chose to disobey God—and the curse began.

Satan influenced Eve, Eve influenced Adam, they both influenced their first son, Cain, and Cain influenced Abel to death! They all continued to influence their sons and daughters—on and on and on it has gone right up to this present modern moment! Like unrelenting ripples on the sea of history, man's influence on one another will continue until we all bump the banks of Eternity.

The moment we are born into this world, we begin the universal process of "becoming." No matter how much space we have in our environment, each one of us will be gently touched or cruelly bumped by those around us—influenced in some way.

That force of influence is either positive or negative. It can either help or hurt, lift up or pull down, encourage or discourage, beautify or uglify, . . . bless or curse.

In the young "spring" years of our lives, our personalities are being delicately molded. The clay of our being is soft and pliable, and we are easily impressed and influenced. Even when we belong to The Lord and claim to love Him, there is a danger of becoming so preoccupied on the "green hills" of pleasant moments that we take our eyes off The Lord.

It is at such a time that our attention can be captured by those around us—the willful, who always want to do it their way—the stubborn, who won't admit when they are wrong—and the lukewarm, who just follow the crowd. They are always nearby and looking for companions. They seem to be so clever and full of fun, always offering something new and different, something better than what we have.

I remember what an elderly lady said to me years ago as she watched me busily tending my four little children. "When they are small they step on your toes, when they grow up they step on your heart." At that time, I was so busy concentrating on the "stepping on my toes" part of our lives that I had not given too much thought to the "stepping on the heart" part. I was smart enough to realize that no matter how I cared for and protected my children, they could not avoid being influenced by those around them—but I did not realize the strength of that influence.

With all the strength and knowledge of the truth that I had, I was determined to teach my children to keep their eyes on The Lord. His influence would be so powerfully wonderful that even when they would be thrown into an evil atmosphere of ridicule and unbelief, they would not fall. Perhaps they may stumble from the force of it for a time, but they would not stay down. Lifted by His strong arm of mercy, they would rise, refined by their pain.

Personally, I had discovered, beyond a shadow of a doubt, that Jesus Christ is the answer to my deep needs—my soul needs! He had lifted me up out of the muddy ditch of despair that I had stumbled into as a teenager. My "ditch" was not filled with immorality, drugs, or even alcohol, it was just . . . empty.

I could see no purpose for the whole thing—life. It seemed to me that no matter how hard I would study and work to succeed, I would still get old, and wrinkled and die. No matter how rich or famous I would become, I would still get old, and wrinkled and finally . . . die. I seemed to bump into that same hopeless stone wall.

One day I attempted to share my growing feelings of futility with my best friend, Cay, who didn't seem to be bothered with the same dilemma. She listened politely as I poured it all out on the way to high school. When I had finished, she said simply, "Esther, you seem to know all about Jesus, but do you know Him?"

Now, I had already told her that my problem had nothing to do with "religion," I had some of that. I was disappointed to find out that she didn't seem to understand what I was going through. But that day at school, I tried to figure out what she was talking about. I liked what I knew about Jesus and the church. I always felt better after going to church because I knew that I had done something good. I believed the Bible. Even as a child I could tell that it was giving wise advice and direction, teaching people to be good. Everybody needed to be good; it just made sense! It was a good book, the church was a good place, and Jesus was a good man—but I did not realize I could know Him personally. How could that be? What difference would it make? Thus, the search began.

One day in a little Baptist church on Harlem Avenue in Forest Park, Illinois, I was introduced to the Savior. Jesus stepped down into that ditch with me and His love lifted me out. He became the supplier of, and not the supplement to, my soul's needs! Never again would I mutter, "What's the use?" He loved me! I was personally important to Him so I knew that He had something personally important for me to do!

I began to realize what happened so long ago on that lonely hill of execution. Fastened to the cross, suspended over the heads of that jeering crowd, Jesus could see forever. Somewhere in the distance, He could see me in my muddy ditch. If in an agonizing moment, so dark and terrible, He would have used His kingly authority to summon His heavenly army to help Him, they would have come in an instant, for they were poised and ready. With the speed of light they could have erased the soldiers and the gawking crowd from the face of the earth.

But . . . what would have become of me? What would become of the millions caught and cut by the jagged rocks of rebellion? What would become of all those sinking in the black mud of guilt and drowning in the raging river of remorse? Who would hear their cry?

Oh, how different it would be today if Jesus would not have finished it. BUT HE DID! In those last agonizing moments of His life, each precious breath must have been a labored gasp. That triumphant, hell-shaking cry, "IT IS FINISHED," may have been only a whisper . . . but that whisper surged through the universe; vibrating from one solar system to another, echoing across the hot rocks and barren plains of whirling planets to the very spot on which we stand.

It is written:

"By the word of The Lord were the heavens made, and all their hosts by the breath of His mouth!"
(Psalm 33:6–Amplified Bible)

"By His breath the heavens are garnished; His hand pierced the (swiftly) fleeing serpent. Yet, these are but (a small part of His doings) the outskirts of His ways or the mere fringes of His force—THE FAINTEST WHISPER OF HIS VOICE! Who dares contemplate or who can understand the thunders of His full magnificent power?"
(Job 26:13, 14–Amplified Bible)

He created the universe with a whisper and He could recreate and restore a fallen race with a whisper!

He is The Restorer of broken things, Jeremiah the prophet said:

"And the vessel that He was making from clay was spoiled in the hand of the potter—SO HE MADE IT OVER, REWORKING it into another vessel as it seemed good to the potter to make it. Then the word of The Lord came to me: O house of Israel, can I not do with You as this potter does? says The Lord. Behold, as the clay is in the potter's hand, so are you in My hand, O house of Israel." (Jeremiah 18:4-6—Amplified Bible)

He is The Restorer of lost joy, King David said:

"Create in me a clean heart, O God, and renew a right, persevering, and steadfast spirit within me. Cast me not away from Your presence and take not Your Holy Spirit from me. RESTORE to me the joy of Your salvation and uphold me with a willing spirit." (Psalm 51:10-12—Amplified Bible)

"He is The Restorer of wasted years, Joel the prophet said:

"And I will RESTORE or REPLACE for you the years that the locust has eaten—the hopping locust, the stripping locust, and the crawling locust. My great army which I sent among you." (Joel 2:25—Amplified Bible)

"If only" are two very sad words. There are some things we cannot change—mistakes of the past, foolish decisions, and angry words. We cry out, "Oh, if only I would not have done that!" "If only I would not have said that!" If only—if only! Regret is an unyielding companion and a thief of peace.

Oh, but THAT CRY! "IT IS FINISHED" meant for us—that the DEBT IS PAID! God piled on Jesus the iniquity of us all. Now, He is able to take the "if onlys" of our lives and use them somehow for something good! Impossible as it surely seems—God is able to restore our battered souls, heal our wounded hearts, turn us right side up, and send us on our way rejoicing! He is able!

JEHOVAH
TSDKENUE
The Lord is My Righteousness
Jeremiah 23:6
"He leadeth me
in paths of
Righteousness
for His Names
sake"

Chapter 5

The rich meadow on that side of the river stretched out lazily in the summer sun and seemed to welcome the flock with open arms. It wasn't long before the eager sheep felt right at home, and they began to spread out over the fertile field.

The restored lambs were on their feet again, Luke and Stubby limped behind the other lambs wherever they went, and the four of them were never far from The Shepherd's side. It is no surprise that they listened carefully for The Shepherd's voice and ran to Him when He called them by name.

Each morning He led the flock a little farther from the river, and they followed willingly, enjoying His abundant provision. But now and then they stood still, curiously studying the great wooded wall that lay ahead of them in the distance.

The inquisitive young rams, becoming more daring, ventured closer to the tall trees and came running back to the flock with breathless reports of strange hoots and howls, and even growls, they heard from the shadowy depths of the forest!

Two old ewes, Timidity and Persnickety, had chilling stories to fit each noise reported. The lambs listened, wide-eyed, to each tall tale, and then rushed to The Shepherd's side.

One cloudy morning, a ripple of nervous excitement passed through the flock. They caught a strange, new scent and all stood still with heads up and eyes turned toward the north-east edge of the meadow, near the entrance of the great forest.

Into their meadow came a stranger and his mixed flock of sheep and goats. A big, black he-goat, with long horns, strutted out in front, proudly displaying that he was the leader of the bunch. The Shepherd stood quietly watching as the stranger approached with his flock.

While the two men spoke to each other, the stranger's flock moved out across the meadow as though it were their very own. Precious watched in awe as the big he-goat and his friends chewed and chomped the tender leaves of the saplings. The stranger's shaggy sheep pushed their way through The Shepherd's flock, challenging anyone who thought to defy them.

By noon the clouds had vanished and the sheep were looking for a shady spot to rest. The goats continued eating everything green in sight. Precious and Satisfied were beginning to worry as they watched the saplings' delicate leaflets disappear.

Suddenly the big he-goat turned and stared at the two frowning lambs watching him. He walked slowly toward them with his head down and horns protruding. Crumpled leaves hung from his mouth, juice ran down his pointed beard, and a pungent odor followed him. It was obvious that he was thoroughly enjoying the fear he saw in their faces. He grinned as he continued to chew noisily. He moved close to the two little ones, who were now trembling, and lowered his hairy head close to theirs.

In a loud, raspy whisper, he said, "I hear your Shepherd is planning a trip into the forest tomorrow . . . what a pity. You could have had a good time with our kids."

Precious and Satisfied just stood there with their mouths open, wondering what upset them most—the sinister face of the big goat, the ominous words that came out of his mouth, or the awful smell!

"Whatsa matter?" the goat asked. "Bobcat got your tongue?"

With this, the munching goats nearby burst into loud, raunchy laughter at the cleverness of the belching bully.

Suddenly, the laughter stopped. The raucous crowd stood still, eyes centered above the heads of the little lambs. Precious recovered a bit of strength and turned slowly. He looked up into the stern faces of the two big horn rams, Steadfast and Unity. They didn't make a sound, but stood there with their necks stretched to full height and their heads turned slightly, so the massive horns could be clearly seen as a stern and silent warning to back off.

The hot summer air became heavy with the strong presence of mutual hostility. No one moved, except Precious and Satisfied, who were shivering so hard it was difficult for them to stay on their feet.

Several moments passed as the group stood staring at each other and then, abruptly, the big goat turned and began walking away.

Steadfast called out in obvious repugnance, "What is your name . . . goat?"

The he-goat turned slightly as he continued to walk and replied in a deep, menacing voice, "My name is Lumpen . . . sheep, and my followers are many and we are strong."

Although Steadfast and Unity recognized the stern warning in his reply, they did not even change expression.

"That's a funny name." Precious said, looking up at Steadfast with a puzzled expression. The two big rams had not moved, they were breathing heavily, muscles still tense, peering at the retreating goats.

"What does it mean?" asked Satisfied.

The childish question seemed to soften the expression on the face of the two strong ones and they relaxed a bit, but they still looked unusually serious.

Unity was the first to reply, "His name describes him as he is—a scoundrel."

Meanwhile, at the far end of the meadow, Stubby, Luke, and Willy had found the stranger's headstrong kids to be willing playmates. The new arrivals brought fresh excitement into their day, for the goats were venturesome and full of fun. The three lambs were captivated by their spooky stories filled with suspense and adventure. They told about the bobcats in the forest who tore little sheep limb from limb and then ate them! They told about great, black birds that swooped down and carried away all sheep that dared to enter their forest. It seemed that each story became more gruesome.

It wasn't long before the stories were being passed on to the rest of The Shepherd's flock and the once peaceful meadow was buzzing with nervous apprehension and suspicion. Timidity and Persnickety were running around telling everyone: "We told you so, we told you so! Didn't we tell you about the hoots and howls and even growls we have heard coming from that dark woods?"

Precious and Satisfied didn't feel like playing or exploring or eating, or anything, because they were busy thinking about what the big he-goat had told them.

"Do you think The Shepherd really is going to take us into the dark forest tomorrow?" asked Satisfied, looking very worried.

"I hope not," replied Precious, frowning an extra deep furrow into his forehead. Neither one had noticed Psalm standing nearby and both looked up in surprise when she spoke.

"There sure is a lot of wondering and worrying going on around here. Have you forgotten to ask The Shepherd?"

Precious realized to his secret dismay that he really didn't want to ask The Shepherd. Since almost everyone else was worrying and questioning, it just felt like the natural thing to do . . . and besides, almost all the big sheep had a nice, deep frown now. He felt very grown up frowning along with them.

"Aren't you afraid of the forest, Psalm?" Satisfied asked.

Psalm looked down for a moment and then replied softly, "Yes . . . yes I am, little one. But I am trusting The Shepherd to take care of the Stalker."

Then she began to sing a song so sweet and clear, that one-by-one the flock pressed in closer to hear her.

It's true, it's true, it's a worrying world,
There's much to be anxious about.
Shadows and noises and rocks that are hurled,
Yes, howls and growls no doubt.

If all alone in this worrying place,
there is much to worry about,
If we never could see The Shepherd's face,
a frown is in order, no doubt.

But The Shepherd is here . . . we're not alone,
He knows what's behind and ahead.
We don't have to live with a frown and moan,
We don't have to travel in dread.
Our Shepherd is strong and mighty to keep,
No foe can withstand His great might.
He promised to care for each trusting sheep,
so rejoice in His way . . . it's right!

It wasn't long before Precious and Satisfied, and the group gathered around were singing the song along with her, and frowns began to disappear.

But suddenly, sharp, raucous voices joined in, drowning out the sweet voices of the singers.

"It's true, it's true, it's a worrying world!
There's much to be scared about.
Tomorrow you will be in the woods
And you will never find your way out!"

They roared with laughter as Precious and the others stood silent.

Then Lumpen's face became slyly serious, and with pretense of concern, he said softly, almost kindly, "We know a way around that dark forest. You don't have to follow that narrow path through the woods. We know a shortcut, a wide road. You all have a special invitation to join us tomorrow morning. I tell you, your Shepherd cannot be trusted . . . Remember, I warned you!" And off they went again.

Precious was confused, for the big goat spoke with such authority and confidence. It would be easier to avoid the forest, and a wide road is much safer than a narrow path. It all made so much sense, but Psalm's song was still in the air and it soothed him to sleep.

The dawn had barely painted the horizon golden orange when Precious awoke. The birds were cheerfully greeting the day and a soft, cool breeze whispered through the branches above his head. He stood up quickly, listening. Yes, there it was again. He heard Emmanuel's voice calling him by name.

Suddenly, yesterday's memory swept over him and he sat down hard, jolted by the frightening thought of the dark forest.

This was the day for the FOREST! He heard The Shepherd gently calling the sheep one by one, by name. They were obediently gathering around Him already, for His sheep recognized His voice and came to Him when He called. The stranger's mixed herd had mingled with the flock during the night, but they did not hear The Shepherd's voice.

After making sure that all of his sheep were accounted for, The Shepherd called them closer to Him and spoke, "I know all about your fear of the forest, and I saw the strangers testing you yesterday; but your love for me and my love for you must cast out that fear, or you will not have strength to follow. Fear has torment and torment produces weakness. I know the way—come, follow me!"

Psalm leaned down and whispered in Precious' ear, "Don't pay any attention to the Stalker, lamb," and she began to sing cheerfully as they fell in step behind The Shepherd. The sun was shining brightly by the time they reached the entrance to the forest. Sure enough, a wide, beaten path led to the left, just as Lumpen had said.

Precious turned and looked back at their meadow. The stranger's herd was up now and moving slowly toward them, the big he-goat once again strutting in the lead. Precious moved close to The Shepherd's side, to see the path on which He would lead them.

"Has anyone walked this way before?" he asked . . . "I don't see a path!"

"Yes, little one," The Shepherd replied, "I have walked this way before, but the path is only opened to those who stay close behind me." He pointed His staff toward two tall pine trees that stood like sentinels at the palace gate. There, between them, lay a narrow, moss-covered path, peacefully winding its way into the shady depth of trees.

By then Lumpen was approaching with his herd. He shouted menacingly to the bewildered sheep, "Remember—I warned you! You can still change your mind. Look here at this nice broad way!"

The Shepherd shook His head sadly, speaking to His sheep as He beckoned to them:

"Enter through the narrow gate, for wide is the gate and spacious and broad is the way that leads away to destruction, and many are those who are entering it. But the gate is narrow—contracted by pressure—and the way is straightened and compressed that leads away to life, and few are they who find it." (Matthew 7:13,14–Amplified Bible)

They all turned to watch the stranger's noisy crowd laughing and joking as they marched down the broad way. Precious felt that many other sheep in his flock were thinking what he was thinking . . . that the strange herd looked so happy and confident and their way really did seem better, a lot more fun anyway.

Satisfied seemed to sense what he was thinking because she said to him, softly, "I guess obedience doesn't always make us laugh, Precious. Sometimes it even makes us cry." Precious nodded and smiled at her, thinking what a wise, little lamb she had become. Her name suited her well.

The Shepherd began to brush aside the leaves and twigs that had fallen across the path with His staff. Little, striped chipmunks scampered away at the disturbance and brown squirrels, clinging to the tree trunks, watched them cautiously, bushy tails flicking from side-to-side.

He walked down the path, using His staff to clear the way. Psalm walked briskly at His heels while the rest followed in a single line. The Shepherd looked constantly behind him at the cautious crowd following Him. After a while, He left the lead to Psalm who was singing His praises out in front, and walked back, reassuring and encouraging the rest of the flock as He went. Unity was about midway down the line and Steadfast was to be the last one. As The Shepherd passed Precious and Satisfied, He paused, smiled, and patted them gently (those five special pats). Precious looked up with grateful eyes and answered in his heart, "Yes, I am loving you, too."

He realized that each step of obedience he took seemed to make him more sure of Emmanuel's love. He tried to imagine life without The Shepherd's nearness. Big, hot tears filled his eyes as he remembered considering Lumpen's broad way.

When The Shepherd reached the end of the line, nearly every sheep had entered the woods. Steadfast was standing at the entrance shaking his head in exasperation, for there, on the broad road, stood Willy, Luke, and Stubby gazing wistfully after the last stragglers following Lumpen and the stranger. They were so preoccupied that they did not even sense The Shepherd's presence. Tapping them rather firmly with His staff, and pointing toward the path in the forest, He said, "Ah, my wandering ones, I have been looking for you. You still have not learned that you are on dangerous ground when you do not follow me!" Startled, the three tempted lambs scampered down the path in to the woods, not even looking back! Steadfast was last in line and The Shepherd knew that all His sheep were safe . . . at the moment.

He now took His place as "rear guard" and His keen eyes carefully surveyed each side of the path as the sheep walked on, for the forest was filled with curious eyes behind bushes and rocks, in the tall grass and even in the tree tops, watching the procession.

It is true that the flock knew that danger existed there, but they saw none. If, for a moment, they could have seen what The Shepherd saw, and could have known what He knew, they would have been easy prey to their predators, for they would have run in terror in all directions. However, their faith in The Shepherd's love kept them walking forward, and fear of The Shepherd's power kept their enemies back.

Gradually the flock began to relax as they walked, for they heard no hoots, or howls, or even growls. All they could hear was the busy chatter of the squirrels as they followed with noisy curiosity. Bright-winged birds flew from branch to branch, chirping and singing as if to announce their arrival to feathery friends ahead. Little, brown rabbits raised their heads from their clover and then hopped away as the flock approached.

Wild flowers bloomed their quiet joy all along the way. Precious and Satisfied squealed with delight as they discovered colors they had never seen before! Warm shafts of sunlight danced around them as the summer wind parted the thick branches above their heads.

It was mid-morning when they reached the quiet stream wandering peacefully across their path. The cool shade around them had made the journey so pleasant not even the lambs were tired, but they all stopped to drink when The Shepherd stopped. The lambs playfully chased each other in and out of the stream while the ewes buried their noses in the red berry bushes beside the water . . . confident that their Shepherd was on guard.

Precious and Satisfied stretched out in the velvety moss beside the still water and looked up at the trees towering above them. Every now and then they caught a glimpse of a patch of blue as the leaves swayed and whispered high over their heads. At that moment, it seemed that there was nothing bad or sad in the whole, wide world.

Suddenly, Precious began to laugh. He laughed so hard that Satisfied sat up and stared at him in puzzled surprise. Not wanting to miss anything, she began to laugh, too. The harder they laughed, the more comical everything became. When Persnickety and Timidity saw them rolling in the grass, they came close and stood looking down at them. The sight of these two made Precious laugh all the harder.

Joyfully exhausted, they were finally quiet. Wiping away the laugh tears, Precious said, "This is the deep, dark forest with spooky hoots and howls and even growls, that they told us about! This is the place that made us worry so hard! This is the place where we didn't want to go—the most beautiful place we have ever seen!"

Satisfied replied softly, "If we would have gone to The Shepherd when we felt the first shiver of worry and asked Him about the forest, He would have told us all about it. Fear sure is easy to catch from the flock, isn't it?"

"And real hard to let go of too!" added Precious. "We should have known that whichever way our Shepherd leads is the RIGHT way, even though it doesn't look like it!

Psalm says that He *is* the way!

Selah

pause and think about it

It has been snowing since early morning and billions of feathery flakes have so weighed down the branches of the pine trees outside my window that many now touch the snow on the ground. The soft, white blanket is very beautiful, but it is making the roads impassable, halting traffic, stopping business, and keeping many people inside.

Now, early afternoon, there are ten inches of snow and more falling. Ian, my husband, has just put on his coat and snow boots to go out and "do his chores." He needs to feed the ducks and check on the condition of his doves in the cage across the stream.

"Do you want to see something funny?" he called to me as he opened the back door.

"Watch Bonnie," he said. Bonnie is our wee black poodle about 12 inches high. I watched from my cozy perch at the window as he trudged through the deep snow. Bonnie leaped off the patio to follow as she had always done before. But this time she sank up to her neck in the snow! Surprised and confused, she jumped and leaped trying to get somewhere. Suddenly, she saw the way to go! Her master was leaving great big footprints that pressed a narrow path right to him. In that narrow trail she followed him all the way to their destination . . . smart dog!

Jesus has pressed down a path for us through the deep snow of life. He blazed a trail through the wilderness and He knows the right way to go.

"Hey, do you want to see something funny?" the enemy of our souls asks his companions in the lower spiritual realm.

"Watch this," and he points to a young man or woman stepping out on their own into the world with no thought of The Master to guide them. Can you hear the laughter from below as the young ones sink down into the immoral slush all around them, as they struggle to get a footing to find the way through the blizzard of life?

Finally they cry out, "Can anybody help me? Can anyone show me the way?"

In response to that plea, God calls His only Son, His Dearest, who shares His glory.

"Jesus, My Son, put on this coat of human flesh and these boots of suffering and submission and go lead them safely through the storm—they have lost their way!"

In obedience, Jesus came to carry out His Father's will. Satan tried hard to stop Him. When the angry crowd cried, "Crucify Him, Crucify Him," the devil thought he had won—it really looked like it. But on the way to Calvary, carrying our load of sin, Jesus made deep, deep footprints of love.

Many scoundrels have tried to cover them up by persecution and ridicule, but they are still there. For centuries men have studied those footprints, criticized them, analyzed them, condemned them, and ignored them—but THEY ARE STILL THERE. Day after day, year after year, multitudes find their way to heaven through Him!

But man is not a "born follower." At a very early age he learns to say, "No, let me do it." We want to do it our way; it looks right:

> *"There is a way that seems right to a man and appears straight before him, but at the end of it is the way of death." (Proverbs 14:12—Amplified Bible).*

Jesus warned us about that way that seems right. He called it "the broad way."

> *"Enter through the narrow gate for wide is the gate and broad is the road that leads to destruction and many enter through it. But small is the gate and narrow the road that leads to life, and only a few find it." (Matthew 7:13, 14—NIV)*

That broad way is crowded for it is popular. There is plenty of room for excess baggage and few restrictions to limit "a good time."

> *"When you follow the desires of your sinful nature, your lives will produce these evil results: sexual immorality, impure thoughts, eagerness for lustful pleasure, idolatry, participation in demonic activities, hostility, quarreling, jealousy, outburst of anger, selfish ambition, divisions, the feeling that everyone is wrong except those in your own little group, envy, drunkenness, wild parties, and other kinds of sin. Let me tell you again, as I have before, that anyone living that sort of life will not inherit the Kingdom of God." (Galatians 5:19-21—NLT)*

When we come to Jesus Christ, we enter the Narrow Gate and we must leave the soiled baggage behind.

> *But now you must rid yourselves of all such things as these: anger, rage, malice, slander, and filthy language from your lips. Do not lie to each other since you have taken off your old self with its practices and have put on the new self, which is being renewed in knowledge in the image of its Creator." (Colossians 3:8-10—NIV)*

Only the constant, almighty presence of The Lord could enable us to do as He says. We can't do it on our own, no matter how hard we try. There are times when we do falter and stumble, but His great love reaches down and picks us up again. He restores us and then once again leads us quietly on in His path of righteousness.

Sometimes the road He chooses for us may lead us into the dark forest of sorrow or suffering. In our distress, we may begin to doubt His goodness, and before we can stop the words, at the threshold we cry, "Oh, God, why?"

No wonder Jesus said, "Few there be that find it"—this narrow way of holiness. But those who do continue on with steadfast endurance, even though their questions are not answered, discover something marvelous—that:

> *"All things work together and are (fitting into a plan) for good to and for those who love God and are called according to His design and purpose." (Romans 8:28–Amplified Bible)*

In some wonderful way, ultimately God makes something beautiful out of it all—but it is in His good time.

Sheep have a problem—they do not have good eye sight. They do not follow their shepherd because they can see him clearly, for they cannot see beyond a few yards. However, they do have good hearing and respond to the familiar sound of the shepherd's voice.

Jesus said:

> *"The watchman opens the door when he has brought his own sheep outside, he walks before them,* AND THE SHEEP FOLLOW HIM BECAUSE THEY KNOW HIS VOICE. *They will never (on any account) follow a stranger, but will run away from him because they do not know the voice of strangers or recognize their call." (John 10:4,5–Amplified Bible)*

What a lesson for us—the sheep are so familiar with the tone and cadence of the shepherd's voice that they cannot be fooled by an impostor! They know that sound which encourages them through the long days and comforts them through the long nights. They go when he tells them to go, and they stop when he tells them to stop. They know his will by the sound of his voice.

Only when we follow The Lord on His narrow way can we really know His will for our lives. Close to Him we listen to His voice as He speaks through His word—guiding, encouraging, comforting, and protecting us against error. The more time we spend WITH HIM in prayer the less chance the impostors have to fool us.

> *"Therefore, I urge you, brothers, in view of God's mercy, to offer your bodies as living sacrifices, holy and pleasing to God—this is your spiritual act of worship: Do not conform any longer to the pattern of this world, but be transformed by the renewing of your mind.* THEN YOU WILL BE ABLE TO TEST AND APPROVE WHAT GOD'S WILL IS—HIS GOOD, PLEASING, AND PERFECT WILL." *(Romans 12:1,2–NIV)*

"He leads us in paths of righteousness—for His Name's sake." Jesus' own glory is involved here. All that He is and all that He promises are on the line. He cannot fail and He will not break His Word. Jesus Himself has become our security on the path!

JEHOVAH
SABAOTH
Commander of The Lord's Army
Joshua 5:14
Yea though I walk through the valley of the shadow of death, I will fear no evil for Thou art with me, Thy rod and Thy staff they comfort me.

Chapter 6

After their brief rest, the flock once again began moving through the forest. By afternoon, the path was gradually leading them upward.

The old ewes were complaining now that they were moving too fast, but The Shepherd continued to urge them on, for evening shadows were slowly gathering around them.

Precious noticed that the choir of birds was quiet now, and the playful squirrels had let the flock go on without them. A strange hush settled over the forest as The Shepherd hurried them on—His rod in one hand, and His staff in the other.

Finally, they reached a small clearing and they could see the blue sky above. There were still tall trees and saplings ahead, but the dense forest lay behind them. The Shepherd gathered the sheep close together to rest while He sat watching, a leather sling in one hand and smooth stones in the other.

A soft, evening shower surprised them as they rested. They turned their eager faces upward to welcome the refreshing moment; but it wasn't long before The Shepherd rose to His feet and called to them to follow. Now, just as suddenly as the rain came, it was gone, leaving behind only the sweet, lingering fragrance of new hope.

Precious playfully bumped a little maple sapling as Satisfied walked by and sent a shower of rain drops on her head. She ducked and laughed, but could not find enough strength to chase him.

Finally, they passed one last clump of trees and were out in the open! A wide field sloped gently downward, and the tall grass leaned and swayed with the evening breezes. They were through the woods!

Standing knee deep in the wet grass, the weary flock began to eat, grateful to be out of the woods, thankful for The Shepherd's protection, and rejoicing in the abundant provision. It seemed that nothing could disturb them now.

But, suddenly from the forest behind them, came a sound that pierced their ears like a sharp thorn. They all looked up, standing very still, listening. There it was again, there was no mistake—it was the cry of the wolf!

"Aaaah-oooooooooh!"

It echoed and re-echoed through the hills around them, and to their horror they realized that it came from the thick forest through which they had just come.

Icy terror gripped each one, as the stalker stepped out of the woods. From the strongest ram to the weakest lamb, they were about to run wildly. But The Shepherd's strong voice rang out clearly over their heads:

"I am here! Do not be afraid of the wolf's voice—I am here! Stay close to me, I am your refuge."

All eyes turned to The Shepherd as He stood in their midst with His arms outstretched above their heads—a calm hush fell upon them.

Precious stood shivering, very close to Satisfied, and said in a rather shaky voice. "Y-yes, it is only a noise! If Emmanuel could protect us from the f-fangs of the w-wolf in the dark woods, He can protect us from the noise of the w-wolf in the open!"

The Shepherd called out again: "Follow me."

The sheep followed Him eagerly, as close to Him as they could get; even Willy, Stubby, and Luke were at His heels!

They walked quickly under the close scrutiny of The Shepherd's eyes, and soon arrived at the place that He had prepared for them long ago. There on the side of the hill was a large circle of rock, piled high; sharp thorn bushes protruded menacingly from the top row of rocks.

Grateful for the sight of safety, the flock pushed into the sheep-cote eagerly, desperately needing a place to rest. They lay down exhausted in the cool grass of their shelter and the shadows deepened into darkness. From the dismal distance, they heard the mournful howl of hungry, disappointed wolves.

Precious looked around at the rocks piled high around him, and he realized that this was the reason The Shepherd had hurried them on. He looked down at his knees that had been shaking so hard and said: "Knees, He did know the way through the forest! He really has been here before! And he slipped confidently close to Emmanuel, whispering:

"Oh, thank you,

thank you,

thank you,

thank you."

By the time all the sheep were settled in for the night, a big silver moon had pushed through the blue shadowed clouds in the darkness above. And now little pin-prick stars glistened and winked at the night wind as it swept the mist away.

There was just enough light to see the large opening by which they had entered the sheep-cote. Precious began to imagine a great line of wolves silently lining up to creep in that entrance when they were all asleep. The stalker sat smiling outside the sheep-cote.

Sure enough, those wolves were offering him that old suffocating fear that he had gotten rid of before, so he moved closer to The Shepherd's side and stood looking up at Him. In a moment, The Shepherd bent down and patted his head gently (those five special little pats) and asked:

"Why are you not sleeping like the others, lambkin?"

Precious' reply burst forth so quickly, it was nearly a shout, as he stared at the ominous hole in the wall.

"There is no door!" he sputtered.

The Shepherd smiled knowingly, and then walked over to the dark opening. He sat down. His back against the big rocks on one side of the entrance, His knees bent and His feet touching the rocks on the other side of the opening. He folded His hands on top of His knees and said simply, "See, I will be the door."

The lamb stood very still looking at The Shepherd in amazement, for He began to realize that any enemy on its way in to kill and destroy would have to go through Emmanuel's protecting presence first!

Overwhelmed by this startling truth, Precious could not hold back great tears of relief and gratitude, and he whispered softly to himself:

"Thank you,

thank you,

thank you,

thank you. . . ."

Precious slept soundly all through the night—right beside the Door. Even though the howls continued and a few growls were added, the flock rested peacefully, confident that The Strong Door was powerful enough to keep their enemies out.

The morning sun was a welcome sight to the travelers. Little brown, speckled sparrows were hopping and stopping in and out among the thorn branches on top of the rocks, watching the newcomers with great curiosity. Magpies flew over them chattering noisily. The danger and fear of the night seemed unreal and unimportant, and the revived flock was ready for a new day.

The Shepherd stood outside the sheepcote looking thoughtfully into the distance below. The meadow that carpeted the hillside was rich and green and provided everything His sheep needed.

Precious was still curled up beside the entrance of the sheepcote; he stretched and yawned and raised his head, looking for The Shepherd. In a moment he saw Him standing alone, studying the valley below.

The sight of Emmanuel rushed such a flood of gratitude and love to his heart, that his eyes filled with tears again. He thought of the long, hard way they had come. He thought of all the foolish things he had done to cause The Shepherd grief. He thought of the five little pats and His smile . . . and then he thought of Lumpen.

What had happened to all the foolish sheep and goats who were following him? Surely they didn't know about all the dangers in the hills?

"Oh, where did that broad way lead them? Where did they spend the dark night?"

He got up quickly and ran to Emmanuel to ask Him.

The Shepherd looked down at the concerned little lamb with an unusual sadness, and then said slowly.

> *"Their shepherds have led them astray and then turned them loose in the mountains. They have lost their way and cannot remember how to get back to the fold. All who found them devoured them. . . ." (Jeremiah 50:6,7a—NLT)*

The deep and profound words spoken by The Shepherd were not easily understood by the little lamb, but Precious could tell by the pathos in His voice that the foolishness of Lumpen and his followers was fatal.

To his surprise, Precious now saw tears glistening in The Shepherd's eyes. Yes, there were the same diamond tears Precious had seen when old Faithful lay in His arms.

"Could it be?" thought Precious, looking very puzzled, "that Emmanuel loves the foolish ones just as He loves the faithful ones?"

At that moment the wise, little lamb realized that he would never really be able to comprehend a love that big . . . no, of course not; he would just have to go ahead and enjoy it!

All that day the sheep grazed in the pasture on the hillside. A cool stream splashed over the rocks and finally slipped merrily into a pond not far from the sheep-cote. The Shepherd laughed as He watched the lambs leaping and kicking up their heels as they headed for the water. The two sisters, Persnickety and Timidity, were moving about trying to keep order, but the happy little lambs didn't pay any attention. In fact, it seemed that the whole flock was rejoicing and celebrating their deliverance from the forest. For at that moment, it appeared that all the danger was behind them. Precious and Satisfied hoped to stay in the hillside pastures for a long time. There was plenty to eat, a safe place to sleep, and beauty everywhere!

Around the sheep-cote, delicate white parasols of Queen Anne's Lace, dipped and nodded in the wind. Bright, yellow poppies, with lace leaves surprised them wherever they went. Tiny hummingbirds hovered and hummed around the honeysuckle, and the little lambs were fascinated by it all. How grateful they were to The Shepherd for leading them there!

To be sure, it came as a surprise when just a few days later, The Shepherd called them together to move on. It was obvious that the sheep were disappointed with The Shepherd's decision to leave that beautiful spot. Willy, Luke, and Stubby were pouting, Persnickety was fussing, and Timidity was crying. Precious and Satisfied were just wondering, but they fell in step right behind The Shepherd anyway.

Unity was moving from sheep to sheep trying to encourage them as best he could, and Precious was glad when Steadfast walked up beside him, because he had some questions. He asked in a loud whisper, "Why are we staying such a short time in this happy place? And where are we going?"

"I'm not sure, little one," replied Steadfast, "but The Shepherd is."

"Oh," muttered Precious, shaking his head as they walked along. "There are so many things that I don't understand."

Steadfast smiled down at the wondering lamb and said, "You are not expected to understand everything, lambkin."

"His thoughts are not your thoughts, neither are your ways His ways, for as the heavens are higher than the earth, so are His ways higher than your ways, and His thoughts than your thoughts."
(Isaiah 55:8,9—KJV)

Precious looked up at him, even more puzzled than before, so Steadfast continued, "Lambkin, His ways are far too big to fit into your little head . . . just go quietly on."

Psalm had been walking just behind the three, listening to their conversation, and now could not help but sing a marching song,

"Now the just shall live by faith;
But if any man draw back,
My soul shall have no pleasure in him."
(Hebrews 10:38—KJV)

As they marched, she sang as loudly as she could and the song was caught up by the wind and swept on ahead of them,

"The just shall live by faith,
the just shall live by faith,
the just shall live by faith. . ."

. . . and the obedient sheep went quietly on.

By late afternoon, they had nearly reached the foot of the mountains, and the way was becoming more rocky. It seemed that they were leaving all the abundant provision behind! The Shepherd stopped, carefully looked about, and then sat down on a huge, gray rock. There was still plenty of grass and shrubs about, so the sheep rested and ate, but it was certain that everyone wished they were back in the beautiful pastures they had left that morning.

Precious was nibbling a patch of grass beside Satisfied. They were both very quiet because they were still wondering about many things, especially the song Psalm had been singing all the way.

Finally, Satisfied broke the silence, "Why don't we go tell The Shepherd about our wondering, Precious? He has always taken care of our worrying—can't He help us with our wondering?"

Precious knew immediately that the little ewe was right (as usual) so they went to The Shepherd together. It didn't take long for him to recognize the mixture of curiosity and doubt on their faces as they stood before Him.

Precious began to explain that they did not understand the marching song.

"Who are 'the just,' and what is 'faith'?" he asked sheepishly.

The Shepherd smiled at the innocent honesty of the lamb; He laid His hand on the head of the wondering one, and said,

"Watch carefully, and I will show you, my Precious. Go rest now."

Precious nodded in agreement, and then looked for a soft spot near The Shepherd's feet. He and Satisfied snuggled up close together and closed their eyes. Their wondering could wait—just a touch from their Shepherd's hand was all they needed, and they drifted off to sleep.

It had been a restless night for most of the flock. They missed the security of the rock sheep-cote, and were still secretly questioning the wisdom of The Shepherd, so of course, peaceful slumber was impossible.

When the first rays of dawn slipped over the mountain and touched their sleepy heads, they were irritated and restless.

When Psalm began her song, many turned away in disgust, but she continued to sing anyway:

"O Come, let us sing unto the Lord;
Let us make a joyful noise to the rock of our salvation.
Let us come before His presence with thanksgiving,
And make a joyful noise unto Him with psalms.
For the Lord is a great God,
And a great King above all gods.
In His hand are the deep places of the earth;
The strength of the hills is His also.
The sea is His, and He made it;
And His hands formed the dry land.
O Come, let us worship and bow down;
Let us kneel before The Lord our maker.
For He is our God; and we are the people of His pasture,
And the sheep of His Hand!" (Psalm 95:1-7—KJV)

Many in the flock paid no attention to the song; but for those sheep who listened to her song of adoration, the morning looked brighter, for the song lifted their drooping spirits.

Precious and Satisfied were eager and ready for the new adventure of the day, and they tried to encourage their grouchy little friends, Willy, Stubby, and Luke, who were sulking.

Cautious was a tall ram who frequently locked horns with Steadfast. He and his ewe, Prudent, were usually at the end of the line when the flock moved forward. They were a fine, intelligent couple, but always seemed to lag behind. At the moment they were really upset because of the direction The Shepherd seemed to be leading them. Now, they really loved and respected their Shepherd, but they felt that at times He was a bit headstrong and took unnecessary chances.

They had called a meeting of the other sheep and were warning the flock of the problems they saw ahead, when Harmony and Unity interrupted them. With an unusually stern voice, Unity commanded:

"Listen! The Shepherd is speaking to us!"

They all turned and faced The Shepherd, anxious to hear what He would say,

"My sheep, hear my voice, and I know them, and they follow me: And I give unto them eternal life and they shall never perish, neither shall any man pluck them out of my hand!" (John 10:27, 28—KJV)

Lifting His rod high above His head, He motioned to the sheep to follow. They began to move toward Him, and the ring of authority in His voice silenced all other voices.

Puffy, white clouds were gathering in the blue morning sky above the sheep as they walked behind The Shepherd. The air was growing cooler, and the way was becoming more and more precarious. The grass now grew in even smaller patches, and the path was narrowing.

The two little lambs had been laughing and playing just behind The Shepherd, and they really had not noticed how everything was changing. Suddenly Precious looked up and gasped in surprise, for they were walking right into a deep valley. The big moss-shaded rocks on either side of the winding path were getting taller and taller until they became great, gray walls that loomed straight up, as far up as Precious could see. Their kind Shepherd was leading them into a dark ravine!

Timidity had stopped short and wouldn't go an inch forward, Persnickety was crying on her shoulder. Cautious and Prudent were trying to organize a group to go back. Willy, Stubby, and Luke were already on their way back, running as fast as they could. Steadfast was at the end of the line, and he stopped them as they tried to scramble by him.

Precious and Satisfied were right behind The Shepherd, as close to His feet as they could get, trembling as they stumbled along. The Shepherd was very serious, glancing from side to side and continually looking back at the flock, His keen eyes examining the cliffs around them. His rod was in His right hand and His staff in His left.

Suddenly, He stopped, and lifted His rod above His head, He let it fly over the heads of the sheep behind Him. It struck the left wall of the ravine just over the heads of Timidity and Persnickety, who were standing still, huddled against the cliff. It struck with such force that it bounced off and dropped between the other sheep. The sharp crack reverberated through the hollow canyon.

The two frightened sheep leaped forward with the others, shocked into obedience! The others around them jumped also and moved more quickly, careful to avoid the rod lying as a still, silent warning in their path.

The Shepherd retrieved His rod quickly and they all moved slowly forward. Precious looked up squinting, longing to see blue sky, but the steep cliffs towered so high above them they seemed to meet at the top. Not a ray of sunlight touched them as they walked that morning, and they shivered in the heavy shade.

Black and green speckled lizards scampered across their path and up the side of the cliff, surprised by the visitors. Precious was sure that he recognized the one with the very long tongue who stared at him and he shuddered at the memory.

The persistent trickle of water from the cliffs above had worn deep grooves in the mountainside, and constantly fed the stream that flowed quietly beside the path. Gradually, the narrow gorge was widening. Rocks of all sizes, broken off from the mountain height, now crowded up against the cliff walls.

Every now and then a black cavern yawned above the rocks beside them, startling them as they passed, so they pushed closer to The Shepherd. They were grateful when He sat down on one of the rocks, as a silent signal for the flock to rest. Feathery fronds of fern framed a crystal pool beside Him, and the sheep gathered eagerly around to drink.

Precious and Satisfied cautiously inspected the thick, green bushes nearby and discovered great bunches of purple berries just waiting to be tasted. Before long, the entire flock had forgotten their apprehension and were happily engrossed in the lush provision of the valley. They hardly noticed that the shade of the valley was getting cooler.

Precious and Satisfied shivered as a chilly wind whistled in their ears. The Shepherd called them together now, and His voice seemed more urgent than usual. The flock responded quickly, for there was a smell of a storm!

Precious was surprised when The Shepherd left the path and began to lead the sheep up a rocky ledge on the side of the cliff. The shivering ones followed reluctantly, keeping their eyes on The Shepherd ahead of them. Precious and Satisfied were as close to His heels as they could get without being stepped on. When he stopped they looked up into the darkness of a black cave!

By now great drops of rain began to fall, and The Shepherd urged them into the cave. Precious stood very close to the entrance, terrified of the mysterious darkness into which The Shepherd had led them, hoping that He would change His mind. Suddenly . . . thet . . . thot . . . splat, sharp pebbles of ice hit his nose.

The Shepherd now stood at the mouth of the cave with His rod outstretched, as each one passed under the rod. Confident that each of His sheep was accounted for, he turned to reassure the frightened creatures, huddled in the darkness.

Knowing exactly what was needed at that shivering, black moment, He began to gather sticks and leaves that had blown into the cave for a moment like this. Soon a bright, crackling fire lit up the gloomy cavern. And the sheep sighed in relief at the sight of it.

The Shepherd moved among them, patting them gently (those five special pats) and they began to relax, reassured and warmed by the light.

Psalm looked lovingly into the face of The Shepherd as He patted her head, and although still shivering, she began to sing a soft, grateful song, that grew louder as the praise gave her strength:

"Your mercy and loving kindness, O Lord
extend to the skies,
And your faithfulness to the clouds.
Your righteousness is like the mountains of God,
Your judgments are like the great deep;
O Lord, You preserve man and beast.
How precious is Your steadfast love, O God!
The children of men take refuge and put their trust
Under the shadow of Your wings.
They relish and feast on the abundance of Your house,
And You cause them to drink of the
Stream of Your pleasures.
For with You is the fountain of life;
In Your light do we see light!" (Psalm 36:5-9—Amplified Bible)

Warmed by The Shepherd's light and Psalm's song, the sheep nestled close to each other, as the storm roared through the canyon. Safe in this hiding place, they could not see the wild rushing river that had once been their quiet stream.

Precious lay quietly with his head resting on The Shepherd's foot, watching the dancing flames of the fire throw grotesque shadows on the walls of the cave. The shadows lunged and leaped all around him, as if to frighten him away, but Emmanuel was there, and Precious was touching Him.

"Anyway," thought Precious, "A shadow is j-just a shadow."

And the little lamb fell fast asleep, whispering softly,

"Thank you,

thank you,

thank you,

thank you,

thank you."

The exhausted flock slept through the long, dark night in safety, dreaming of the morning with sunshine and blue skies. But the dawn arrived unannounced in the cave, almost hidden in the shade of the valley.

Only the embers glowed on the floor of the cave now, as the sheep began to stir. There wasn't a sound to be heard except the steady drip, drip, drip from the entrance of the cave. The Shepherd was moving slowly among the sheep, calling them softly by name.

Precious looked toward the entrance of the cave and wished they would all hurry out of the dismal place. Finally, he stretched and stood up, and nudged Satisfied who was just opening her eyes.

"Want to see what it looks like outside, Satisfied?" he asked, yawning.

"Shouldn't we wait for The Shepherd?" she replied.

"We won't go far, come on." Precious said, heading for the entrance.

Satisfied followed, quite easily convinced, for she too longed for the fresh air. She was just a few steps behind Precious when he stepped out on the rock ledge above the valley.

Suddenly, she fell back in terror as a great black form lunged at the helpless little one standing outside, so near the safety of the cave. A vicious snarl punctured the early morning stillness as a wolf's sharp teeth sank into the silky neck of the little lamb! The vicious animal's rough claws scratched and grated on the rocky ledge as Precious struggled, but the iron jaws held him tight. With lightning speed, the big, gray wolf shot down the narrow ledge, leaping from one great rock to another with the helpless body of the precious lamb dangling from his mouth.

The surprised flock cried out in fright and confusion. Satisfied lay limp on the floor of the cave, gasping in fright. In an instant, The Shepherd was out on the ledge. He could see the wolf with its valuable prize, racing toward its lair in the ravine.

Precious lay in a pitiful heap on the damp floor of the gray wolf's den. His eyes were closed, and his head throbbed, scalding pain pulsed through his body. He could hear the voracious animals growling and snapping at each other, greedy to get the first bite. The air was putrid and heavy with savage breath as they snarled over his head. He could not move for he was completely paralyzed with pain and terror.

The big gray had dropped Precious on the den floor only moments before, but to the bleeding lamb it seemed as though hours had passed, for he slipped in and out of consciousness. At this moment, the pain was gone and he found himself running through the mountain meadow with Satisfied, he saw The Shepherd's smile and felt His touch (those five special pats)—in the next moment, the terror of the darkness lunged upon him once again like a hot tidal wave. The pain boiled and twisted deep inside his little frame.

Suddenly, a great shout of anger exploded into the cave and echoed back into its dark depths! Like a missile, a stone whizzed over Precious' head, and then another and another! The startled wolves yelped in pain as they clawed and scrambled over each other, trying to retreat back, back into the murky darkness of the cave.

There in the entrance of the den stood The Shepherd, muscles taut and eyes flashing. With His staff He struck the stone wall of the cave again and again, the hollow cave amplifying the sharp cracks as He charged into the lair!

But, the big gray stood his ground over his prey. His head was lowered and his back arched, his fur bristled, snarling lips quivered over white fangs. Poised to spring, he stared in angry defiance at his challenger.

Suddenly, The Shepherd raised His rod above His head and sent it flying. It shot through the air and smashed into the wolf's head! The beast fell to the ground with a thud, and lay very still—beside Precious.

The wounded lamb could not open his eyes, but he felt himself being lifted, gently, oh, so gently. He wanted to cry out in pain, but he found no strength to make a sound, for his tangled coat was stained red.

The Shepherd held the bleeding lamb in His arms, with His right hand pressed firmly over the gaping wound in the little one's throat. He moved quickly down toward the swollen stream on the floor of the canyon. He kneeled down and gently washed the jagged cuts in the icy water. Precious did not stir for he was far away in an unconscious mist, and felt nothing.

Now and then he heard The Shepherd's voice as they walked through the valley. He tried in vain to open his eyes, or make some sound; but there was no strength left in him, for the wounds were deep and had nearly drained all life from him. He lay very still, pressed close to The Shepherd's heart. Psalm sang softly as she walked beside The Shepherd:

"The Lord is my light and my salvation;
Whom shall I fear?
The Lord is the strength of my life;
Of whom shall I be afraid?
When the wicked, even my enemies, and my foes,
Come upon me to eat up my flesh,
They stumbled and fell!
Though a host should encamp against me,
My heart shall not fear,
Though wars should rise against me,
In this will I be confident!
And now shall my head be lifted up above mine enemies round about me.
Therefore, will I offer in His tabernacle
Sacrifices of joy;
I will sing;
Yea, I will sing praises unto the Lord!"
(Psalm 27:1-3,6—KJV)

Even though the song was faint and far away, it was able to pierce through the heavy mist, and penetrate the lamb's thorn-wall of pain to reach his heart; for the words were powerful and strong and kept perfect time with the heartbeat of The Shepherd.

Selah

pause and think about it

It would be easier to understand the Shepherd's "paths of righteousness" if they always led through sunny meadows and beside quite streams–but they don't. Deep ravines and valleys are also on the map.

It is not possible for sheep to stay on one pasture and grow properly, for their provision is soon used up. It is necessary for them to move on–it is for their good. But, unfamiliar territory is frightening and sheep are not brave. The Stalker, Fear, is their constant companion.

They are afraid of heights, hunger, strangers, insects, snakes, other animals, swiftly moving water, thunder, lightning, loud noises, the sight of death . . . and even shadows. The safety and peace of these timid creatures depends upon their shepherd. He is strong and accustomed to danger. He knows the strategy of the enemies and is well able to protect his flock if they obey Him. He knows the way through the valley.

In the "valley of the shadow of death" we discover, like the sheep, that we are not so brave either; because something big–very big, has interrupted the light rays and we cannot see. In that darkness, the stalker, fear, would carry us away into despair, were it not for the presence of the Good Shepherd.

Strange . . . that this experience in the shadow could be so lonely in such a crowded place. There has never been a time when that valley was empty, and the footsteps of millions have made it very deep.

Many times in my 50 years as a pastor's wife, I have been shaken from my busy routine by a phone call that cut through the quietness of my day. Such a call came from Carolyn. Even during difficult times, her voice had always sounded like there was a smile behind it somewhere. But this time it was different–now there was a sob!

"Esther . . . this is Carolyn . . . Turk had a heart attack . . . Oh, Esther . . . He's dead! . . . Turk is dead!"

One morning she and her husband had been enjoying the sunny security of an anticipated ordinary day. Suddenly, like a tidal wave, the whole family was swept into the valley of the shadow of death. So quickly, from his favorite chair in the living room, Turk stepped into the valley of the shadow with the speed of a deep breath, and into the presence of his Lord.

Just one deep breath and he was through the valley! But not so for Carolyn and her son and daughter. That valley cast a very long shadow on those left behind. It is hard to even imagine that any blessing could come out of this sadness, but a few months after this shattering experience Carolyn told me, in a voice filled with quiet emotion, that in the midst of her sorrow, a gentle peace had strengthened her and carrier her through.

This is what the wise psalmist meant when he wrote:

"Blessed (happy, fortunate, to be envied) is the man whose strength is in You, in whose heart are the high ways to Zion.

Passing through the valley of Weeping (Baca, they make it a place of springs; the early rain also fills the pools) with blessing.

They go from strength to strength (increasing in victorious power); each of them appears before God in Zion." (Psalm 84:5-7—Amplified Bible)

Those who know their Saviour, The Shepherd, before they reach that parched valley are the ones who are able to "make it a place of springs."

There are days of warmth and safety when we are sheltered by our family and friends. The sun is shining and we are enjoying the security of familiar territory. From this pleasant mountain slope, we may notice suffering and death from a distance and feel very sad—but it does not change the course of our life, and we are glad.

But, sooner or later our own feet will touch the shade. A few days ago it was our turn once again. For years, as pastors, my husband, Ian, and his brother, Alastair, had knelt at the bedside of many suffering saints and then stood at their open grave. From God's wonderful Word they were able to offer sure hope and warm comfort to those whose lives were forever changed by the death of that one so dear.

With all their love and sympathy as pastors they walked as far as they could in the valley with the grieving families; but, soon they had to let go of their hands, for it was impossible to enter completely into their grief or lift the shadow in which they were walking.

Alastair and his wife, Ginny, had 49 fruitful years, working side by side in the ministry. Although retired, they were still busy preaching and teaching. Their four children were grown and had homes of their own. Ginny had great delight in her grandchildren and she was looking forward to the soon arrival of a new granddaughter who was to be named after her.

One Wednesday morning she and Alastair went shopping for a new rocking chair. She picked out one that fit her just right, and as she tried it out in the furniture store she pictured the little one nestled in her arms. The chair was carefully placed in its special spot in the living room, and every time she passed it that day she must have smiled with anticipating joy. It represented the hope of a new life about to enter the world.

That evening Alastair went off to speak at the prayer meeting of a church near by. Ginny usually accompanied him, but this evening she was tired. It was decided that she would stay home and rest.

Alastair knew what to expect as he drove home from the meeting that night. Ginny would be busy in the kitchen as usual. They would sit down at the table and he would enjoy the sandwich that she always had waiting for him after the service . . . as usual. They would discuss the meeting and then he would move to his favorite chair in the den to watch the evening news, while she finished in the kitchen . . . as usual.

He was in familiar territory, and it was comfortable. . . . He knew what to expect.

He had no idea that he was on his way into the valley. As he drove into his garage he noticed "something" lying in a heap on the edge of the driveway. He walked over to examine it and to his horror he discovered that it was his beloved Ginny, lying on the cold cement.

Without warning, Alastair and his family plunged into the valley of the shadow of death, leaving forever the fragrant, familiar every day routine order of their lives. "A massive cerebral hemorrhage," the doctor said. Now, Ginny, the one everyone depended upon, the wise Bible teacher, the efficient nurse, the tender wife, the loving mother and grandmother was silent–never to regain consciousness on this side of heaven. She was deep in the valley of the shadow of death and we could not get to her. We clung to this one source of comfort–she was not alone there . . . Jesus was with her.

Her time in the valley lasted only a few days—and then with one final heartbeat she stepped triumphantly into the glorious radiance on the other side of that last obstacle—death . . . into the open arms of the Lord God Almighty, the One she loved so dearly. All shadows were left behind forever.

But, not so for the family left behind in the valley. Shadows don't hurt, they say . . . this is only half true. A shadow cannot crush the body like a mudslide, but it can fall upon us and smash open our heart, filling it so full of tears that our soul nearly drowns.

The valley is a deep place for us. The psalmist knew. He said,

"Deep calls to deep in the roar of your waterfalls; all your waves and breakers have swept over me.

By day the Lord directs His love, at night His song is with me—a prayer to the God of my life."
(Psalm 42:7,8–NIV)

God's waves and breakers "sift us." God uses our sorrow to "sift out" superficial things that clutter our lives. Our values change; those things that were once so prized and necessary for our happiness are not important anymore, and our attention turns to things that matter most.

Then in love, God "lifts us" and gives us a song in our night.

"But you, O Lord, are a shield for me, my glory, and the lifter up of my head."
(Psalm 33:3–Amplified Bible)

God promises:

"Weeping may endure for a night—BUT JOY COMES IN THE MORNING."
(Psalm 30:5–Amplified Bible)

His word is like a piercing shaft of light that brings us a glimmer of hope in the deep darkness of our valley. He is the only one who can do this!

So . . . whether the valley leads to our death, to the death of our beloved one, or to the death of our dreams—it is always meant to lead us to higher ground; the supremely highest—heaven, or the next to the highest here on earth—"heavenly places"—very close to the One behind it all, God!

"But God, who is rich in mercy, because of His great LOVE with which He loved us, even when we were dead in trespasses, made us alive together with Christ (by grace you have been saved) and raised us up together and made us sit together in the heavenly places in Christ Jesus." (Ephesians 2:4-6–NKJV)

Isn't it wonderful to realize that God wants us to be "TOGETHER" with Him? It is not until we discover for ourselves the "realness" and nearness of God that we begin to understand that life is leading somewhere. We are not merely leaves blown by the wind, floating for a few moments in the sunlight, then dumped on a pile in darkness!

God has a plan and a purpose in all that happens to us, even though we cannot see it with our limited vision.

"For I know the plans I have for you, declares the Lord, plans to prosper you and not to harm you, plans to give you hope and a future. Then you will call upon me and come and pray to me when you seek me with all your hearts—I will be found by you," declares the Lord. (Jeremiah 29:11-13–NIV)

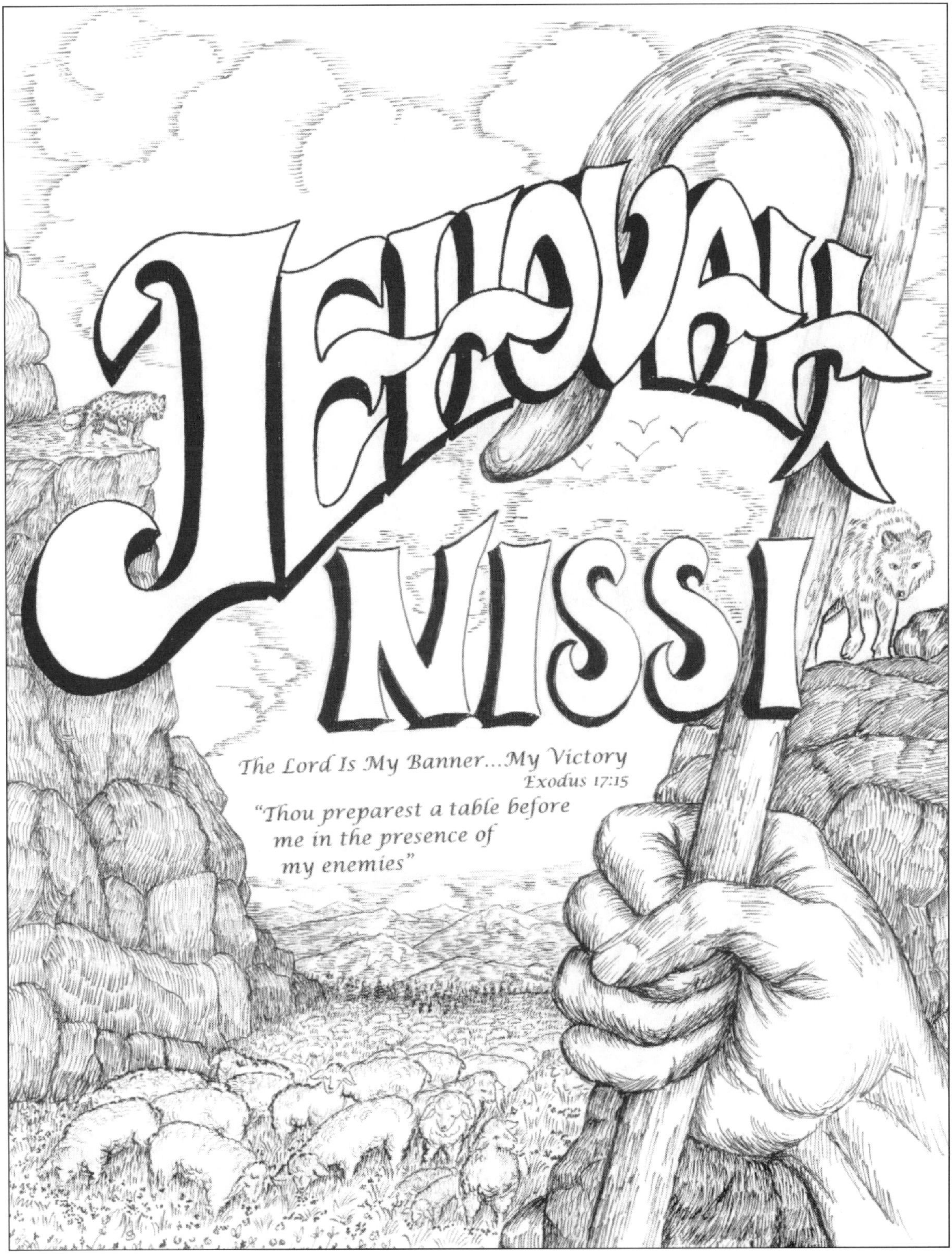
JEHOVAH
NISSI
The Lord Is My Banner...My Victory
Exodus 17:15
"Thou preparest a table before
me in the presence of
my enemies"

Chapter 7

The valley was strangely peaceful now after the storm. The footsteps of the sheep behind The Shepherd kept perfect time with the gentle trickle and splash of the fountains that now flowed from the rocky canyon walls.

Colorful little birds in the bushes chirped loudly in surprise, and flew upward as the hungry flock discovered the berries under the wet leaves.

The sheep now knew that the valley had enemies they could not see or hear. They knew they had no might or strength against the great company that surrounded them—so they kept their eyes on The Shepherd. He had led them into the valley, and only He could lead them out.

It was a surprise to the flock to realize that such a fearful and foreboding place could provide such lush abundance to nourish them. Water even flowed from the rocks! They began to realize that they were walking through a place where the dangers were never greater, but the provisions never richer.

Precious lay quietly in The Shepherd's arms, and did not stir even when bright shafts of sunlight danced on and off his face. Satisfied jumped joyfully into each splash of sunshine in the path, eager to feel the warmth on her back. Somehow, she had feared that they would stay forever in that valley, but now she saw that they were just passing through. The walls of the canyon were behind them now and, at last, they were moving up. Tall mountain laurel leaned over gently, offering shade as they passed. Never had the flock appreciated the bright sunshine as they did now, and they certainly did not want to avoid the warmth of its rays. In fact, the long, dark hours in the valley had given them a new appreciation for everything in the light!

The Shepherd led His flock upward slowly, for he carried the injured lamb in His arms. In that coveted place, Precious did feel safe, but not warm. He shivered in sullen silence as though he were still in the shade of the valley, for deep in his heart a different kind of pain was growing more intense. It was the dull, throbbing pain of doubt and disappointment.

Strange foreign thoughts, like chilly wind swept through his clouded mind, whispering as they passed:

"How could this have happened to you? Don't you belong to The Shepherd? WHY did He not keep you from the wolf's mouth?"

But no answer came. He tried to recall sweet moments before the valley. He tried to remember the five special pats. He tried to remember The Shepherd's smile, but he could not.

There it came again: "Is He really as strong as you thought?"

"Does He really love you?"

Great hot tears welled up in the eyes of the oppressed little lamb as he struggled in the wild whirlwind of unanswered question. The wise Shepherd could sense the storm going on inside His little lamb, and gently pressed him closer to His heart.

The rocky mountainside gradually became steeper now, and the sheep were growing weary. It was time to rest the flock, so The Shepherd carefully lowered the suffering lamb to a patch of soft grass beneath a laurel bush.

The interruption silenced the questions for a few moments, and Precious was grateful. He opened his eyes and tried to lift his head; but could not, so he just lay very still, squinting at the patches of blue sky between the laurel branches.

He whimpered when the nagging, unwelcome questions began again:

"Why did The Shepherd not keep you from the wolf's mouth? Why?—why?"

Just then, the smiling face of his little friend, Satisfied, appeared above his head, and he heard the soft voice of Psalm close beside him. Hot tears suddenly filled his eyes and softly overflowed; he blinked quickly hoping not to miss a moment of this welcome sight. Surely Psalm would be able to answer his painful questions. He tried to summon strength to speak, but only a faint, hoarse, whisper of a word came forth. . . . "WHY?"

Psalm leaned down close to his face, sympathizing tears glistened in her eyes, "Ah, little one," she said, gently, "you are still in the wolf's den, aren't you?"

Satisfied's smile disappeared, and she gazed at Psalm with bewildered surprise, for she did not understand. Precious was there with them, safe and loved, wasn't he? She tried to smile once again as she leaned over Precious and looked into his eyes, but there was no response. It seemed as though he did not even see her, or the blue sky, or anything around him.

It was true. Precious squeezed his eyes tightly shut as the stench and snarls of the wolves' lair rushed over him. He couldn't seem to get out of the cave. The way seemed blocked by the avalanche of unanswered questions. A painful realization was slowly rising to the surface . . . deep down in his heart Precious felt anger toward The Shepherd. The pain of this added wound was more than he could bear and he cried out in anguish. It was not a loud cry, for that was yet impossible; but it was loud enough to reach the ears of The Shepherd and in a moment, He was there.

He gathered the quivering lamb in His arms and held him close to His heart, knowing the storm of emotions in His frail, little one. After a few moments He began to speak softly:

"Precious, when you were born, I gave to you a very valuable gift, although I knew that it had the powerful potential to hurt you, even to take you away from me. Because of my great love for you, I wanted you to have it so that your love for me would not be forced . . . I gave you the will to choose."

Precious listened intently, for Emmanuel's words were like medicine to him:

"I am a refuge and a fortress to you when you abide under my shadow, when you stay close to me. My obedient sheep follow me, they stop when I stop, and wait until I lead them on. Precious lamb, when you choose to run ahead of me, you are always in danger. Your adversary, like a roaring lion, roams about looking for someone to devour!"

As The Shepherd's words flowed like warm oil into the open wounds of his heart, he slowly began to realize what had happened. He had slipped out from under the shadow of The Shepherd, away from his protection and into the enemy's ambush.

A new awareness of The Shepherd's love began to appear before his tired eyes. In spite of his own foolishness, his Shepherd had followed him into the cave of the wolf, fighting for his life!

Amazed at the mercy he now saw, overwhelmed with the gratitude he now felt, he let go of the anger that had kept him prisoner in the cave, and he slipped out into the sunshine, whispering:

"thank you,

thank you,

thank you,

thank you,

thank you,

thank you."

. . .very softly, of course.

The Shepherd continued to carry the healing lamb as they moved up the mountain, for the way was becoming more steep and rocky. From the valley below, menacing sounds of their old enemies reached their ears, and everyone knew that the wolves were following. The Stalker was also following and each distant howl sent ripples of fear through the flock.

Satisfied kept as close to The Shepherd as possible, but she could not help but hear the nervous complaining and fretting going on behind her. She found herself listening more closely to what they were saying.

"Remember the wide pasture on the other side of the great woods? Oh, how I wish we would have stayed there!" said Persnickety shaking her head.

"We were safe there," Timidity added, "and there was plenty of food."

In a voice quivering with emotion, Prudent asked: "Why must we climb so high? We were well satisfied on lower ground."

Willy couldn't forget Lumpen and his laughing crowd and said: "I'll bet they are having a great time down below. I wish I would have gone with them."

Luke and Stubby nodded their heads in agreement.

The murmuring behind Satisfied piled heavily upon her, and she began to lag behind, feeling more and more uncertain and afraid. She was relieved when Psalm moved up beside her and smiled knowingly.

"It is difficult not to listen to them, isn't it?" she said, tossing her head toward the grumbling group.

With downcast eyes, Satisfied nodded her head in agreement.

Psalm continued: "It sure isn't easy to climb to higher ground, but it will be worth it, little lamb. If you listen to the murmurers around you, you will gradually grow weaker, so keep your ears open to The Shepherd's voice.

Encouraged by her own words, Psalm began to sing so that all around her could hear:

"As for God, His way is perfect;
All the Lord's promises prove true.
He is a shield for all who look
to Him for protection.
For who is God except the Lord?

Who but our God is a solid rock?
God arms me with strength;
He has made my way safe.
He makes me as surefooted as a deer,
Leading me safely along the mountain heights."
(Psalm 18:30-33—NLT)

The beautiful, marching song gave Satisfied new energy and she moved quickly up beside The Shepherd, singing her own song:

"I'm pressing on though the way is steep,
And the murmurer complains and groans,
I will grow weak and want to weep,
If I listen to all of their moans."

The Shepherd smiled and leaned down and patted her head proudly (those five special pats) because although the song was simple and a bit off key—the words were true.

The sky was growing overcast as a heavy mist drifted down from the heights. It was getting more difficult to see ahead now, and the sheep were becoming more aware of the strange sounds, not only from the valley below, but from the mountain above. They stumbled on in silence, too scared now to murmur.

The Shepherd had climbed this mountain many times before and knew it well. He was heading for a cavern that He had prepared months before. His flock was hungry and tired and desperately needed a safe place to rest. Just up ahead, hidden in the mist, was their refuge on the mountainside.

He pushed aside two large rocks, He led His anxious sheep into the place He had prepared for them. Soon, a fire crackled cheerfully on the cavern floor and the frightened sheep began to relax, comforted by its warmth and light.

Not far away, a thin, hungry cougar crept silently, almost invisible, in the gathering fog. In the very presence of this strong enemy, the helpless sheep feasted peacefully on The Shepherd's provision . . . unafraid.

Precious nestled close to Satisfied on the soft bed of straw near the campfire. He was able to raise his head just a bit now, and even managed a faint smile now and then as Satisfied chattered on beside him, trying to make him laugh.

The Shepherd was busy examining His weary sheep, patting them gently and massaging their tired legs. He cleansed and soothed their scratches and cuts with His oil and carefully removed the twigs and thistles from their coats. Precious watched Him intently as He tenderly cared for the bedraggled bunch, who were feeling very sorry for themselves.

"Why in the world does He love them so much?" he thought, "They are unclean, and unlovely . . ." He groped for a word to describe what he saw, "and unworthy, that's the word, unworthy of His love and attention." He sighed and leaned back on the straw.

"There are so many things I do not understand," he thought, "I have so many 'whys' and they get me all mixed up."

Suddenly, he realized that he had not heard a word Satisfied had been saying to him. He looked into her contented face and felt that she possessed something he had lost.

Satisfied frowned as she noticed the puzzled expression on his face, and asked:

"What's wrong, Precious?"

Precious responded softly, almost whispering, "What do you do with your 'whys'?"

"What 'whys'?" she asked tilting her head to one side.

"What do you do with the things you don't understand, I mean." replied Precious.

The little ewe was silent for a moment, it seemed as though she was looking far off somewhere. Finally she sighed and said,

"When the Shepherd took me out of the butcher's cold hands, and held me close against His heart, I felt something warm and wonderful. I didn't know what it was then, but I do now . . . It was His love. He loves me, so I know that he will explain to me what He wants me to understand, and I must trust Him for the rest. . . . HE MUST LEAD AND I MUST LEAN."

The words sounded far too simple to be true, but Precious knew she was right. All the apparently senseless struggle and pain could have some value in his life if it taught him to LEAN ON THE SHEPHERD!

Could this be what The Shepherd had promised to show him . . . "The just shall live by faith?"

Into his heavy darkness burst a shaft of light—**FAITH IS THE LEANING!** . . . Yes! The little wounded one smiled, placed his head on the soft straw, and fell into a deep, peaceful sleep.

In the morning, long, golden shafts of sunlight filtered into the cavern and past The Shepherd standing in the narrow entrance. One by one, the sheep stood up and stretched, refreshed and ready for the journey.

The Shepherd lifted the leaning lamb up in His arms once again, and stepped out into the fresh air. His keen eyes searched the mountainside, cautiously examining the bushes near the trail upward, then, with a wave of His staff, He began the morning climb.

The flock followed obediently, invigorated by the cool currents of Alpine air. The wind whistled through the gnarled branches of low twisted trees, that seemed to cling in desperation to the mountainside.

Mid-morning, they came upon a narrow waterfall, splashing joyfully from the heart of the mountain into a pool that persistence had carved out of the rock. It was a welcome sight to the thirsty sheep and they eagerly crowded around it.

The Shepherd placed Precious down on a patch of green herbs not far from the pond; Satisfied scampered up beside him, glad to be near her little friend. They did not notice the wide-winged, sharp-eyed vultures silently circling above the flock; but The Shepherd's keen eyes were upon the scavengers, and the hungry birds knew it.

After a rest, that seemed far too brief, The Shepherd picked up Precious once again and called to His sheep to follow. Many were surprised and a bit reluctant to move on for they could have been quite content on this level and had little desire to climb higher. They grumbled and dragged their feet until Psalm began her song:

"The Shepherd calls us higher;
Come along!
Forget what lies behind you,
It is gone!
Reach for that which lies before,
For ahead there's so much more.
Even if the lions roar,
And the vultures soar,
Leave the lowlands far behind
and press on!"

So they did, encouraged and reminded of truth they had forgotten . . . they pressed on.

Through the afternoon, they moved up slowly but steadily, pausing now and then to nibble the tufts of grass peeking out cautiously from behind the rocks. Their fleecy coats were covered with tiny droplets from the misty shoulders of the clouds that leaned over the mountain.

Suddenly, a ripple of excitement spread through the flock, for they realized that they had reached the summit! With a burst of new energy of joy they stepped out upon the mountain tableland. A banquet was spread before them as far as their eyes could see in the gathering mist.

Out in the broad, open pasture, The Shepherd stood smiling as the hungry sheep buried their faces in the grass. Looking out over the banquet table, Satisfied cried out in amazement:

"Oh, Precious, it was worth it! The valley was so dark and scary, and the climb was so rocky and steep, but look where our Shepherd has led us. . . . It is worth it all! It is worth it all!

Precious stood quietly drinking in the beauty of the magnificent moment. He looked toward the weary sheep now eagerly feeding on the abundance, and remembered their discontented voices just a short while before on the path.

"Oh!" he thought, "What they would have missed if they had given up on the climb! The best was yet to be!"

Just then Steadfast moved closer, his mouth was full and busy, but he was still able to manage a large, juicy grin.

"Wonderful!" he said, munching cheerfully.

"Wonderful!" agreed Precious, "It's lucky for us that The Shepherd found this beautiful place."

Steadfast gulped, and his head popped up as though he had been stung on the nose by a yellow jacket in the grass.

"Lucky! Lucky, did you say?" He shouted so loudly that all the other sheep looked up in surprise.

Steady bent very low, his nose almost touching Precious' trembling nose, and said sternly:

"Lucky" is not one of The Shepherd's words. Surely you do not think that we have stumbled upon this bountiful banquet by mere chance—No!" shouted Steady, stretching himself to his full height.

Precious was thankful that Steady didn't wait for an answer to his question, because he didn't have one.

"It was planned! Every step of the journey was planned by our Shepherd. Before the first spring breeze touched us, He made the long journey across the wide river, through the dark forest and glen. Aye, He climbed this very mountain to make it ready for us."

He stopped speaking abruptly and glanced furtively over his right shoulder, and then the left, as though he expected something to pounce on him. A shadow of fear swept across the big ram's face and the two lambs shuddered. Steady's voice was soft and low as he continued:

"We cannot even see our enemies, in the trees, behind the bushes, in the grass, and even in the holes in the ground! They are well hidden from our eyes—but they are here."

He paused and smiled before he continued: "But, The Shepherd sees them, and they fear Him!"

Precious and Satisfied relaxed and breathed a deep sigh of relief for this welcome and comforting news. They both looked out over the prepared pasture where the flock was feeding peacefully, oblivious to predators, the problems, and this profound truth.

Looking at their Shepherd moving among them, they said softly:

"Thank you,

thank you,

thank you,

thank you,

thank you!"

Back on the steep path over which they had just come, the cougar crouched low and watched with fierce, hungry eyes. Behind the distant rocks, the mountain lion paced slowly back and forth. But the sheep grazed peacefully and Psalm sang joyfully, for The Shepherd was right in the midst of them.

"I sat down under His shadow with great delight,
And His fruit was sweet to my taste.
He brought me to the banqueting house,
And His banner over me was love!"
(Song of Solomon 2:3,4—KJV)

Selah

pause and think about it

There is a lovely phrase, recorded from the past, that echoes through my heart—"Come, wash up . . . suppertime!" Mom would open the back door just wide enough to call and wave to us as we played in the back yard. It was a welcome call, because by that time of the day my two brothers and I were hot, tired, bothered and hungry. It meant that it was time for all the kids who had wandered into the yard, to go home. This invitation was for the family only.

We would dash in to the nearest sink and wash our hands as fast as we could, eager to get to the table first. There it was—all spread out before us, nothing fancy, or more than enough, but good—just what we needed.

I had done nothing, but respond to the invitation and eat. My mother's loving hands had done it; it was all prepared for me. It brought me pleasure; but as a child, I did not realize that my enjoyment of the meal also brought pleasure to my mother.

Years later, with children of my own playing in the back yard, I smile when I remember them dashing to the supper table. I enjoyed seeing them take pleasure in that meal because I knew that they were tired and bothered by the childish business of that day. I knew what they needed and I had prepared that meal in anticipation of their needs. When they were satisfied . . . I was satisfied.

There is a tender meal-time experience that John recorded in his gospel. Jesus had been betrayed, arrested, beaten, humiliated, tried . . . and finally crucified. It all happened so quickly; one day the disciples were sitting at the table with Him, enjoying the sunlight of His presence; and the next day they were dragged into the valley of the shadow of death.

All those wonder-filled days of miracles, healings and teaching were over. It was all over! Jesus was dead and buried. Their hopes and plans for the future were smashed under the big rock that sealed that tomb. They were disillusioned, disappointed and defeated.

Suddenly they received the astounding news that Jesus was alive! He had risen from the dead as He said He would! During the next forty days, He appeared to them, at different places and at certain times, to prove the reality of the Resurrection and to comfort and reassure them. Jesus knew that it would take time for all of these amazing facts to soak in, for their minds were overloaded with the wonder of it all.

The disciples had once felt confident and united with Jesus beside them every day, teaching and guiding them. It would be different now. What were they supposed to do now?

One day Peter decided that he had to do something. He said to six of his friends, "I'm going fishing." At least he felt confident to do that. It sounded like a good idea and they responded, "We are coming with you."

But even in that familiar territory nothing seemed to go right. They fished all night long and caught nothing—not one fish. By the time the dark water sparked with the golden rays of the rising sun, they were worn out. Another disappointment was added to their collection. Nothing was going right for them and they couldn't seem to get out of the shadows.

Tired and discouraged, they headed toward land. As they approached they could see someone standing on the shore watching them. In the early morning stillness, His voice carried loud and clear over the water.

"Boys, have you caught anything?"

Only another fisherman would be down at the lake at that time of the morning, so they were not surprised at His interest. Perhaps they could spare Him some wasted energy and time trying to fish that morning. They shouted back an emphatic "No!" To their surprise He then told them just where the fish were at that moment.

"Cast your net on the right side of the boat and you will find some." Now, they were exhausted and it seemed like a waste of time and strength. But the stranger's voice was hard to ignore. Reluctantly they took his advice. To their surprise . . . He was right! Their net came in full and running over.

"That's what Jesus would have done," Peter thought. "It is the Lord," he cried as he dove into the water. His guilt-strained heart longed to be in His presence.

That revelation of the Lord's intimate knowledge and awareness of their personal needs was a tremendous lift for those troubled men. But the tender experience that followed, as they pulled into shore was different. Jesus laid aside His royal robe of omnipotence and became their loving friend—He was preparing breakfast for them there on the shore!

The One who had made the sea, the shore, and the fish was now cooking for them; like a father would do for his hungry children. He knew what they needed on the sea—His guidance. He knew what they needed on shore—His love.

Jesus prepared a table before them in the presence of a hostile world; in the presence of their doubts, discouragement and fear—the enemies that were paralyzing them.

Centuries have gone by since that seaside breakfast, but those same enemies are with us. Jesus still stands on the shore watching us as we sweat and strain on the sea of our circumstances. When finally, worn out and discouraged, we notice Him. He calls out, "Child, have you found the peace you were looking for?" If we are honest and respond, "No," then He tells us the right side to cast our net—the right place to look:

"Come to me, all you who labor and are heavy-laden and overburdened, and I will cause you to rest; I will ease and relieve and refresh your souls." (Matthew 12:28–Amplified Bible)

It is a DAILY invitation and FRESH provision. God supplies one day at a time, persistently teaching us to depend upon Him, not monthly, or weekly, but daily—one moment at a time. Our needs are brand new every changing moment.

"Blessed be the Lord, who DAILY loaded us with benefits, even the God of our salvation." (Psalm 68:19–KJV)

"Because of the Lord's great love we are not consumed, for His compassions never fail. They are NEW every morning; great is your faithfulness. I say to myself, the Lord is my portion; therefore I will wait for Him." (Lamentations 3:22-24–NIV)

How amazing! The Lord is my portion! Not only does He daily prepare His table before us, and invite us to COME—but He offers HIMSELF AS OUR PORTION:

"The Lord is my chosen and assigned portion, my cup, you hold and maintain my lot." (Psalm 16:5–Amplified Bible)

The disciples were as amazed as we are at this astounding offer. That last night before the crucifixion they ate together.

"Jesus took bread, gave thanks and broke it, and gave it to them saying, 'This is my body given for you; do this in remembrance of me.' In the same way, after supper He took the cup, saying, 'This cup is the new covenant in my blood, which is poured out for you.' " (Luke 22:19, 20–NIV)

What a mystery! What an incalculable expense! How often we forget what it cost the Father to prepare that table for us in the presence of our enemies. It is hard to imagine that anyone who is hungry would ignore or reject the loving invitation to COME and EAT, but it is going on right now!

Jesus told a story about a special suppertime in Matthew 22:1-14. A king was planning a wedding banquet for his son. This would be a "once in a lifetime" experience for all of the guests. Not only would there be a royal abundance of the very best food, but they would have the privilege of fellowship with the king and his family! What an honor to be invited to such a happy occasion.

Preparations had been started months ahead of time so that every detail would be taken care of. Finally, the food was all prepared and ready to be served. The servants were sent out to tell the guests to come—all was ready! The table was set with the best china, the rolls were hot, the main course out of the oven, and the musicians were ready to play their instruments!

Now, those who were invited had been given plenty of time to prepare themselves for the celebration. I can imagine all the excitement in each home when they realized that the KING wanted their presence at the banquet!

They were looking forward to their new clothes, for it was the custom in that day for the king to provide each guest with a beautiful robe. They must have brushed up on the proper etiquette for the presence of royalty. They must have marked off the days on their calendar in anticipation.

When the servants finally came with the long-awaited news that it was all READY–what a flurry of excitement there must have been in each home. Certainly no one wanted to keep the king and his son waiting, and they certainly didn't want to miss anything! They must have rushed to the palace.

NO . . . surprisingly sad to say, these were not the reactions or actions of the invited guests! When the servants summoned them, they refused to come! The gracious king perhaps thought that there was some misunderstanding, so he sent the servants back to tell them about all the delicious food on the menu—all seasoned to perfection.

But, there were no misunderstandings—they simply did not want to come! Some paid no attention at all to the invitation, ignoring the servants. Some laughed at the invitation and made fun of the servants. Some were just too busy and preoccupied with their farmyard and business; they had work to do and didn't have time.

All of these reactions were startling and hard to believe, but there was an even more terrible reaction down the road. Some of the invited guests grabbed the servants, beat and humiliated them, and finally, killed them!

When the servant who had escaped reported what had happened, the king was furious! He sent soldiers out to put the murderers to death. He even burned their cities.

The table was still set, the food was still ready; but the guest list was now changed.

"Go out to the main roads and invite anyone you meet," the king commanded.

Soon the banquet hall was filled with hungry people who were thrilled to leave their meager provisions and poverty-stricken tables. Can you hear the "oohs and ahs" as they dropped their tattered clothes and slipped into the velvet and satin robes the king provided? They were going to eat with royalty and wanted to be dressed properly.

When their host, the king, came in to welcome his guests, he received another surprise. One of those seated at the table preferred his own tattered clothes to the robe that the king had provided. It was as if he was saying, "I want to enjoy the food, but I want to come my way. I like my rags." He had accepted the invitation but refused this king's complete provision.

This stubborn and rebellious attitude was judged rapidly! He was bound hand and foot and tossed out into the darkness.

God has set the table for us in the midst of all the problems of pain, failing health, sorrow and the evil around us. He is providing just what our hungry souls need—LOVE, FORGIVENESS, MERCY, HOPE, PEACE, JOY, PURPOSE, GUIDANCE, COMFORT, AND THE SECURITY OF HIS PRESENCE.

But we must come to His table on His terms. We must slip out of the rags of our own righteousness and allow Him to clothe us in the white robe of His righteousness.

What an invitation . . . "Come, sit down at the table and LEAN ON ME, I WILL SUPPLY YOUR EVERY NEED" Wow!

JEHOVAH
M'KADDESH
"I am the Lord,
who makes you holy"
Leviticus 20:8
Thou anointest
my head with oil
my cup runneth
over

Chapter 8

Exhausted by the long journey and the excitement of the day, Precious fell asleep quickly. But even before the sun had made its aureate announcement of a brand new day, Precious was wide awake in avid anticipation of his first morning in The Highlands.

The dew-drenched pasture glistened in silent serenity before his eyes, and he wanted Satisfied to share the wonder of it all.

He nudged her gently and waited for her to open her eyes and remember where she was. She blinked her eyes and stretched lazily; but, when she looked up into Precious' excited face smiling down at her, she jumped up!

"Oh," she whispered, "I thought it was a dream! But we are really here, just as The Shepherd promised!"

The air was cool and fresh in those early morning moments and their breakfast was spread before them. The whole flock seemed jubilant having finally reached the abundant heights, and they didn't seem to mind when the lambs frolicked among them. Even Timidity and Persnickety smiled patiently at them as they bumped and teased.

Precious and Satisfied had eaten almost as much as they could hold now. In that coveted condition and in that special spot, they really should have been completely happy; in fact, they were both making a real effort to rejoice. However, they were discovering that they did not have the mountain top to themselves. Relatives of the minuscule menace were there, too! Flies and gnats came in single file and swarms, swooping and stinging, tickling and tantalizing, just as they had done in the lowlands.

Precious was really surprised and found it difficult to hide his disappointment; not only because of the unwelcome presence of these pests; but also, for the unpleasant discovery of the sharp thorns and prickly burrs hidden in the bushes.

The truth was that Precious and Satisfied, along with many others, had assumed that everything would be different when at last they reached the coveted higher ground . . . that somehow they would be above and beyond the common cares and mundane muddle of the lower level.

The noisy pests stubbornly buzzed in their ears and tickled their noses no matter how hard the lambs rejoiced. They were both trying hard to ignore the noisome pestilence when

Unity and Steadfast approached them, smiling pleasantly. Noticing the luscious berries above the lambs' heads, they paused and asked politely:

"Do you mind if we enjoy some dessert with you, lambs?"

Without waiting for an answer, they began to eat the berries too high for the lambs to reach. By this time Precious and Satisfied were so irritated that they were in no mood for smiles and courteous conversation, so they just stood quietly, eyes blinking and noses twitching.

But as Precious watched the big rams munching and smiling, he noticed that something was missing . . . something definitely was not there . . . absent as absent could be!

"Why aren't you bothered with the FLIES?" he blurted out, almost shouting.

The two rams looked down at the lambs and their flies; but since their mouths were very full, it took a few moments of serious chewing before they responded. Finally, Steadfast leaned down a bit, shook his head, and replied:

"Why *are* you bothered with the flies?"

Obviously irritated by the ridiculous question, Precious shouted: "Because they are here, that's why!" But needing an honest answer, he tried to control himself as he continued:

"Will we never get away from bothersome things no matter where we go or how high we climb?

"Nope," replied Steady, nonchalantly reaching for another berry. But then, seeing their chagrin, he sat down beside the lambs (and their flies, of course) and added:

"You see, lambs, there are just too many of them and they are everywhere; they come in all shapes, sounds, and sizes."

He squinted his eyes and tilted his head to one side just a little bit, and said:

"Let's see now, there are annoyances, vexations,

aggravations,

nuisances,

irritations,

provocations,

exasperations,

(He took a deep breath) disturbances,

harassments,

persecutions,

frustrations,

worries,

and troubles . . .

. . . to mention just a few."

"Oh dear," whispered Precious as he shook his head sadly, "What in the world can we do with all of them?"

"We must make use of them," Steady replied quietly, "Our opponents can become opportunities."

"Opportunities?" the lambs blurted out in a dumbfounded duet.

Steady and Unity threw their heads back and laughed in delight at the opportunity to talk about opportunities.

"Yes, lambs," Steady said recovering his composure.

"It's a worrying world, you see; but any problem that is given to The Shepherd, becomes an opportunity for us to see how great He is!"

The Shepherd! Suddenly the two lambs realized that they had done it again . . . they had taken their eyes off The Shepherd, even on that mountain top, where the air is so clear and The Shepherd so near.

At that moment, He was in the midst of His sheep tending to their needs. When the breathless lambs dashed up to him, He quietly drew the two bothered ones close to Himself, for He knew their needs before they arrived.

They both stood very still in grateful anticipation as The Shepherd began to pour His own special, soothing oil upon them. It covered their defenseless heads and seeped gently through their silky fleece, comforting and soothing as it trickled down their shoulders and legs.

In those peaceful moments, touched by The Shepherd's hands, and anointed with His oil, their joy was full to the brim. It overflowed into a grateful and determined song for their tomorrows:

"We shall bend our head each morning
For Your tender, loving touch;
Troubles ambush without warning,
And they weaken us so much.

Oh, we need a fresh anointing
Of Your precious, soothing oil,
For our strength is disappointing,
We grow weary of the toil.

Like a gentle summer shower,
Pour Your blessing from above.
Fill our barren lives with power,
Fill our empty cups with love!"

Selah

pause and think about it

It was a gracious custom in the East for a host to welcome his guests with special gestures of hospitality. He provided a basin of water at the door and a servant to wash the guests' feet, soiled by the dusty road they had just traveled. His guests would then be anointed with a fragrant oil that soothed and refreshed. All of this demonstrated the host's pleasure of their company and his desire for their comfort.

During the meal, the guests were given a cup of choice wine. If the host filled it until it overflowed, he was telling them that they were very welcome and while they were in his home they would be liberally treated. But, if their cup was not filled to the brim, they received a message that they should not stay too long—their presence was politely tolerated.

Jesus was invited to dine at the home of a religious leader named Simon. All these gestures of hospitality were missing. Simon gave little attention to his guests' comfort.

There was much activity as the meal was being served, and the other guests were busy talking and laughing. They didn't notice a woman as she slipped into the room. She was a woman of the street, with a soiled reputation, and was certainly not invited. But, her longing to see Jesus was greater than her fear of ridicule. She made her way to the place where Jesus reclined at the table and fell down behind Him—at His feet, sobbing.

It is obvious that she knew more about Jesus than the others in the room. She had heard His tender teaching and had seen Him touch the sick and miserable—healing and restoring them. His purity and strength drew her to Him. Her stained and restless soul desperately needed that touch. From her agony the tears flowed, falling on the feet of the Son of God . . . what an honored place for her tears.

Using her long hair as a towel, she gently wiped the Lord's feet, and then kissed them. At that tender moment Jesus must have been the only one aware of what was happening—but, when she broke the little flask of costly perfume, everyone looked up . . . for the fragrance filled the room.

This must have been a tense moment. This interruption was not on the program! The host was disgusted and muttered to him, "What is she doing? Who let her in? Why is she wasting that expensive perfume? Doesn't Jesus realize who this woman is? If this man is a prophet, he will not allow this!"

The Lord knew what was on that man's mind, and He saw the pride and hypocrisy embedded in his heart. He knew all about the woman too, her sordid past, her regrets, her broken heart, and her sorrow for her sin.

Jesus' reply to the man's thoughts must have surprised everyone in the room. He did not reprove and embarrass the woman—but He turned His attention to the failure of the man.

> *"Then turning towards the woman, He said to Simon, 'Do you see this woman? When I came into your house, you gave me no water for my feet, but she has wet my feet with her tears and wiped them with her hair.*
>
> *You gave me no kiss, but she from the moment I came in has not ceased (intermittently) to kiss my feet tenderly and caressingly.*
>
> *You did not anoint my head with (cheap, ordinary) oil, but she has anointed my feet with (costly, rare) perfume.*
>
> *Therefore, I tell you, her sins, (many as they are), are forgiven her—because she has loved much. But he who is forgiven little loves little. ' And He said to her, 'Your sins are forgiven!'" (Luke 7:44-48–Amplified Bible)*

Our God is The Magnificent Host of heaven and the universe. We are invited to come to Him—to be His guest at His table. . . . How astounding! This would be more conceivable if He treated us with "polite toleration," like Simon did, but He calls us with tender love and compassion and desires to take care of our every need! He does this in spite of our unsteady devotion and vacillating wills. . . . No wonder He compares us to sheep.

Since it was impossible for our finite minds to understand such infinite love, He had to come down and stand right in front of us. Jesus is God's love PROOF! He said to His disciples long ago, and keeps repeating to us today:

> *"I came that you may have and enjoy life, and have it in ABUNDANCE (to the full, till it OVERFLOWS). (John 10:10–Amplified Bible)*

Not just life—but abundant life—overflowing life; just as a shepherd leads his flock to higher ground, Jesus leads us. This high pasture is a place of plenty, prepared for those sheep who follow the shepherd and walk in trust and obedience.

But, we discover as we follow the Lord, that no matter how high we climb, no matter how close we get to Him in this world, we don't leave all the problems and irritations behind us somewhere. They can't follow us into heaven, but as long as we are here—they are here.

Jesus informed us that trials are inevitable.

"I have told you these things, so that in me you may have (perfect) peace and confidence. IN THE WORLD YOU HAVE TRIBULATION AND TRIALS AND DISTRESS AND FRUSTRATION—but be of good cheer (take courage, be confident, certain, undaunted)! FOR I HAVE OVER-COME THE WORLD. (I have deprived it of power to harm you and have conquered it for you.)" (John 16:33–Amplified Bible)

So we are to:

"Consider it wholly joyful, my brethren whatever you are enveloped in or encounter trials of any sort or fall into various temptations,

Be assured and understand that the trial and proving of your faith brings out endurance and steadfastness and patience. But let endurance and steadfastness and patience have full play and do a thorough work—so that YOU MAY BE (PEOPLE) PERFECTLY AND FULLY DEVELOPED (WITH NO DEFECTS) LACKING IN NOTHING." (James 1:2-4–Amplified Bible)

The tried and refined disciple, Peter, encouraged the troubled Christians of his day. They were going through suffering and persecution and needed some answers!

"In this ye greatly rejoice, though now for a season, if need be, ye are in heaviness through MANIFOLD TRIALS, that the trial of your faith being much more precious than of gold that perisheth, though it be tried with fire, might be found unto praise and honor and glory at the appearing of Jesus Christ." (1 Peter 1:6–KJV)

We are waiting for the sight of our wonderful Saviour! But—in the meantime our faith is being tested . . . for a reason. When a lump of gold is dug out of the earth, it is thrown into a hot furnace, it doesn't stay the same lump . . . something is happening. All the dross, the impurities, rise to the surface as scum. It is no longer hidden in the lump, it is now revealed and removed . . . AND WHAT IS LEFT IS PURE GOLD.

God is in the process of refining us through "manifold trials." "Manifold" means "many colored." Difficulties come in every color of the rainbow; and like a sunrise, they are always changing.

But here is a wonderful truth–just as there are "manifold trials,"—THERE IS ALSO "MANIFOLD GRACE!"

"As every man hath received the gift, even so minister the same one to another, as good stewards of THE MANIFOLD GRACE OF GOD." (Peter 4:10–KJV)

MANY COLORED TRIALS—MANY COLORED GRACE!

Our Lord is The Great Color Coordinator of the universe! Everytime we see a rainbow, God's signature in the sky, we are reminded of His Grace. His loving kindness can match any hue, shade or tint that comes into our life—not way ahead of time, but just when the color shows up.

A rainbow appears in the clouds only after the rain. The rain of pain, sickness, sorrow and trouble splatter on our souls and we sometimes feel that the clouds of discouragement will never leave. But, clouds are only part of earth's lower atmosphere. Above them, there is a constant, never dimming LIGHT SOURCE . . . Jesus! To remind us of His constant and never dimming love, He splashes a glowing arc of color across the sky right over our heads! It's a promise . . .

"I do set my bow in the clouds, and it shall be a token of a covenant between Me and the earth. And it shall come to pass when I BRING A CLOUD over the earth that the bow shall be seen IN THE CLOUD." (Genesis 9:13,14—KJV)

He is the One who brings the clouds . . . so that we can see the Rainbow of His Grace in this lower atmosphere. But, earth's downward pull is constant, the world around us tries to claim our attention, and we very easily become earth-bound. Our gaze turns downward and we don't even notice the Rainbow.

Jesus knew that this would happen to His disciples. As long as He was with them, they were looking up at Him. But, what would happen when the time came for him to leave them? They were to represent Him in the same world that crucified Him! They would be in dangerous territory on an impossible assignment.

It was really raining—clouds of fear and despair surrounded them, so Jesus painted His Rainbow on their clouds:

"And I will ask The Father, and He will give you another Counselor, WHO WILL NEVER LEAVE YOU. He is The Holy Spirit, who leads you into truth. The world at large cannot receive Him, because it isn't looking for Him and doesn't recognize Him . . . BUT you do, because He lives with you now and later will be IN YOU. No, I will not abandon you as ophans — I will come to you." (John 14:16-18—NLT)

And He did just as He said! The terror of the crucifixion must have blotted all His wonderful promises—oh, but after The Resurrection—the sun came out! They were anointed with the fresh oil of the Holy Spirit and they were never the same. So saturated were they with His presence that earth's gravity seemed to have lost its power to pull them down. In the midst of hostility, threatenings, imprisonment, they stood firm in their faith. Even death could not silence them. Their words ring out loud and clear to us today from the pages of our Bible.

Now, we too bend our heads each morning for a fresh anointing of oil. Only The Holy Spirit Himself can enable us to live holy lives in such an unholy world. His name is Jehovah M'Kaddish, "the One who makes us Holy." We can hear the echo of Jesus' words on that hill in Galilee . . .

"Lo, I am with you always, even unto the end of the world!" (Matthew 28:20b–KJV)

Surely goodness and
mercy shall follow me
all the days of my life
EL SHADDAI
ALMIGHTY GOD
ALL-SUFFICIENT STRENGTH-GIVER
NOURISHER ... SATISFIER
Genesis 17:1

Chapter 9

Precious was growing. Now, when he stood beside the other sheep he did not have to stretch and strain to see over their heads. His spindly legs, that had buckled and bent so easily, sending him sprawling amidst the laughter of the flock, were now strong and his steps were steady and firm.

There was another evidence of growth that was not as easily detected, but had great significance. He had learned in the early spring that The Shepherd loved him—for He had surely proved it; and Precious' infant love for The Shepherd had continued to grow. As long as he could remember he had been awed by the strength and power of The Shepherd—this had never been a problem to the growing lamb.

However, through the summer days of his life Precious had been content, at times, to be out of The Shepherd's immediate presence. Just knowing that he was somewhere near, and could be found if needed had seemed to satisfy the lamb—but that had changed. The growing lamb now realized that there was only one place where he felt really safe and satisfied. He was no longer content to admire Him from a distance, he must be very close—touching Him.

There was also another benefit that Precious discovered while leaning on The Shepherd. He could hear all the instructions and advice he gave the other sheep if he listened. Yes, without even asking a question, he was learning. This happy discovery produced a song:

I'm leaning and listening and learning
In this very special place.
I'm in the shadow of the Shepherd,
So close I can see His face.
I'm leaning and listening and learning,
Knowing that there will always be more.
Not content to watch from a distance,
I'm close to the one I adore!

I'm leaning and listening and learning,
Oh, why didn't I enter before?

I have tried to climb through the window,
When I knew that He was the door!

Yes, I'm leaning and listening and learning,
Expecting the oil He will pour,
Enjoying the peace of His presence,
And training my spirit to soar!

At Emmanuel's side, Precious watched the golden hues of autumn spread quietly across the meadow and over the mountains in the distance. Every tree and bush seemed to agree with the change. He had dearly prized the myriad shades of summer's satin greens, but he could not deny the beauty that was unfolding before his eyes.

The growing lamb had always looked upon change as an insidious intruder in his life. It seemed that he fell so deeply in love with the present moment, that he could not bear to let it go. But, no matter what he did to hang on to it, it always changed its appearance and left him.

But now, looking at his days from under the shadow of The Shepherd, his eyes were protected from the searing rays of the sun, and he could see more clearly. He could see that although everything around him changed, The Shepherd didn't. His love and care were changeless! No matter what the season or the color of the trees—He was the same!

Little did the growing lamb know that all the truth he had learned in his Spring, Summer, and Autumn were about to be tested—for there was a new season ahead. One day, while leaning and listening, Precious heard a new word . . . Winter. The Shepherd spoke about the cold wind that would soon whistle around them, and the crystals that would hang sparkling from the bare branches of the trees. He described the silent, white blanket of snow that would cover the dry grass and rocks, hiding the ground.

Precious was listening intently to all the chilly, winter words when the stalker approached him from behind and whispered softly:

"It sounds kind of scary, doesn't it? What if you can't find anything to eat?"

He began rattling off as many "What if's" as he could, just as quickly as he could, for he knew that he was in The Shepherd's territory and wouldn't be able to stay long.

Sure enough, Precious turned and spotted him crouching behind him, and he leaned even closer to Emmanuel, who, of course, had heard it all. Completely disarmed by the expert leaning of the growing lamb, the defeated foe disappeared into the chilling, autumn mist . . . but he was not far away.

Precious and Satisfied were noticing that their generous meadow had become reluctant to provide the nourishment they needed. So they were not surprised when The Shepherd called the flock together one cool morning to tell them that they were moving on.

The maturing flock was still not free of their concern about the future, so they crowded as close to The Shepherd as they could. The chill of uncertainty was in the air and the Stalker was in the mist. The Shepherd knew His sheep well and understood their frail feelings, so He spoke very gently to their upturned faces.

I will not in any way fail you nor give you up nor leave you without support, I will not, I will not, I will not in any degree leave you helpless, nor forsake nor let you down—relax my hold on you! Assuredly not! (Hebrews 13:5b–Amplified Bible)

Assuredly not! The strength of His voice and the certainty of His promise swept over the heads of the helpless sheep like the rays of the sun after the rain. As the warmth of His words penetrated their minds, the weakness of uncertainty left them, and they were ready to go.

With renewed confidence and courage, the sheep fell into step behind The Shepherd. They were eager (at the moment) for the journey, even though they had no idea where they were going or what lay ahead on the other side of the mountain.

However, the Stalker was also confident. He followed from a distance, hidden in the fog, sure that he would have his chance to speak later on.

The Shepherd moved slowly in the somber light of the early morning. The gray clouds hung low above their heads and sent a cold drizzle of rain down upon them. He kept a close watch on the aged ones, for the way was wet and slippery and although the spirit was willing for the journey—their flesh was weak.

Precious and Satisfied were full of energy and eager to move ahead. But every once in a while, they looked back over their shoulders hoping to catch a glimpse of their familiar autumn pasture. It was all hidden from view, wrapped in the mist of hours passed.

Persnickety and Timidity were grateful when The Shepherd paused beside a quiet stream. They seemed a bit out of breath; but, managed some loud, long sighs when they saw their friends, Cautious and Prudent, walking toward them.

"I know that The Shepherd knows best—but, I think it would have been wiser to wait until the clouds lifted," Cautious said softly as he sat down beside Timidity, who was looking quite pathetic.

"Yes," agreed Prudent, "This is not good weather to be slipping and sliding on the side of a mountain." Then she added quickly, "But, of course, The Shepherd knows best."

They all nodded in agreement and said, almost in unison, "Of course," then sat in sullen silence looking back into the distance from which they had come.

After giving His sheep a time of rest and quietness to regain their strength, The Shepherd motioned for them to follow, and they were on their way again.

By afternoon, a blustery wind had swept the heavy clouds away and uncovered the sun. Its welcome warmth soon dried the fallen leaves on their path and the sheep shuffled along on a crackling, ruffled carpet. Each great gust of wind sent a shower of red and gold leaves dancing and swirling around them, as if to encourage them onward.

As the shadows grew longer and darker, the sheep moved more slowly. Precious and Satisfied had expended their abundant energy jumping into every convenient, and inconvenient, pile of dry leaves and chasing the bright ones that drifted down from the trees. They were exhausted and their legs were weak.

What a relief it was when The Shepherd led them off the path and close to the stony shoulder of the mountain. There, overhanging rocks formed a shelter, wide enough for the whole flock. They rested for the night close to The Shepherd and each other—in the safety of the cleft of the rock.

The sheep awakened early to a faint rumble of thunder in the distance. The air was heavy with fog and a strangely solemn stillness. The crickets that were usually in concert at dawn were silent. The few leaves left on the trees were still.

Precious stretched and yawned. Seeing The Shepherd standing outside the shelter, he rose quickly and walked to His side. He could see that The Shepherd was deep in thought as He studied the landscape around them.

When The Shepherd reached down and patted Precious' head (those five special pats), the lamb realized that his Friend's face was more serious than usual.

One by one the sheep awakened and came to The Shepherd, sure that He would soon be calling them to follow Him. He showed them the berries and pale, green grass hidden under the leafy carpet just outside the shelter. They began to eat.

Willy, Stubby, and Luke were greatly enjoying the treasure hunt, and each one tried to outdo the other. They were moving farther and farther away from the flock in their hungry excitement, and could only faintly hear the voice of The Shepherd as He called the sheep back to the shelter. They looked up for a moment and saw the flock returning to the cleft of the rock; but they continued eating, sure that He would call again later.

The flock was surprised when The Shepherd interrupted their breakfast. His voice had a ring of unusual urgency and they obeyed quickly. The very moment they reached the shelter, the ground beneath their feet began to shudder. They all turned their eyes toward The Shepherd, who was listening intently to the deep and ominous rumble that was growing louder. This thunder-like sound was not coming from the sky above their heads, but from the ground beneath their feet!

Suddenly, the earth began to shake and groan. The bewildered sheep cried out in terror as they were tossed about like the autumn leaves in the wind, and thrown to the ground.

Great rocks heaved and grated beneath them with a deafening roar from the abysmal center of the earth. Jagged boulders, ripped from the mountainside, plunged from the heights, crashing around the entrance of their once safe shelter.

The convulsions seemed to subside for a few moments only to break forth in an even more violent upheaval! Gradually the wild shaking grew less and less and less . . . the subterranean struggle seemed to be over . . . now, there was silence.

Choking, blinding dust swirled in the air and then slowly began to settle down upon the terrorized sheep, sprawled on the ground.

They lay still, unable to move, numb with fright. It was not until Precious heard Emmanuel's voice that he began to move. He lifted his head, whimpered softly and opened his eyes as he heard The Shepherd shout: "Don't be afraid, I'm here."

One by one the stricken sheep lifted their dusty heads, stunned and bewildered. Their terrestrial trust had been shattered! That which seemed so secure and too strong and firm, ever to be shaken . . . HAD BEEN SHAKEN!

Ah . . . but that voice, strong and clear, gave new strength to their feeble knees and they slowly rose to their feet. The Shepherd moved among them, speaking softly now to each one, and patting them gently (those five special pats). His touch reminded them that even though everything in their world was out of place . . . He was there . . . and somehow everything would be all right.

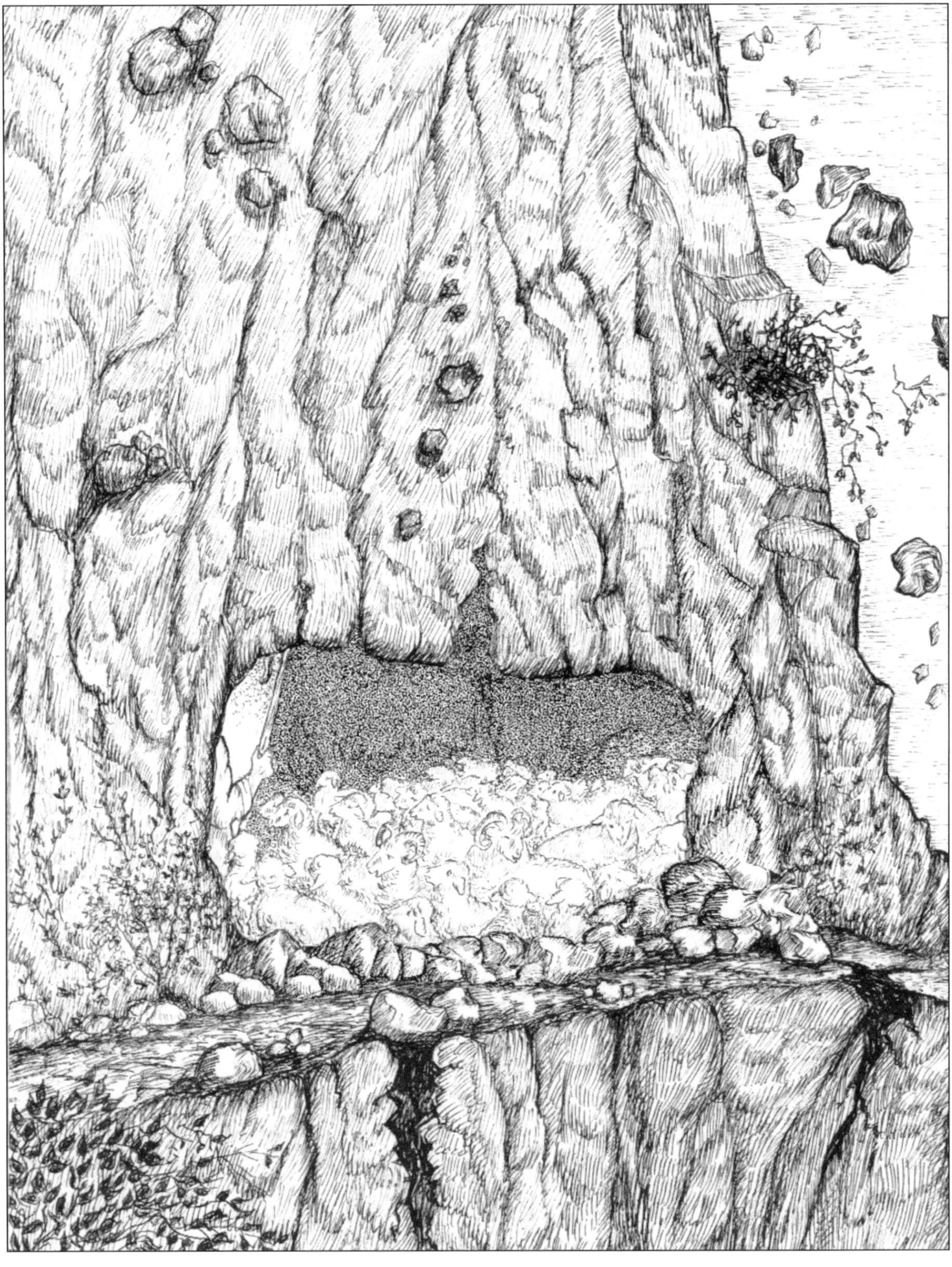

Now, a song would also seem out of place in that discordant moment, but even though bruised and bumped by the disaster, and covered with the descending dust, Psalm began to sing! At first she could hardly be heard, for her voice was weak; but as the words penetrated the chaos around and within, she began to sing more loudly:

"God is our refuge and strength.
An ever-present help in trouble.
Therefore we will not fear,
Though the earth give way
And the mountains fall into the heart of the sea,
Though its waters roar and foam
And the mountains quake with their surging.
Selah" (Psalm 46:1-3—NIV)

And the disturbed and dusty sheep paused . . . and thought about it.

After The Shepherd made sure that His flock was safe, He turned from them and walked out into the open air. All could see His great concern. He cautioned Steady to keep the sheep in the cleft of the rock, for the danger was not yet over—and three careless sheep were not in the safety of the fold!

The terrain outside the shelter was completely changed! Great boulders lay all around, split in fragments. Trees were bent and splintered. A deep, jagged crevice stretched out into the distance.

The Shepherd made His way quickly to the open crater and peered into its shadowy depths. Without a moment's hesitation He began to climb down into the yawning crevice, for His keen eyes spotted His three unconscious sheep on the broken rocks below, nearly covered with dirt.

He knew that He had to work quickly for the aftershock was sure to come, and the sheep would soon be buried. One by one, He carried them up to the safety of the cleft of the rock.

He carefully examined them to make sure their bones were not broken and then brushed away the dirt and bits of rock clinging to their bodies. As He poured His oil on their cuts and bruises, they began to stir. They cried out in pain as they tried to lift their heads. The Shepherd leaned down and spoke softly in their ears, reassuring them of His love and their safety. He caressed them gently . . . and they relaxed.

Precious stood nearby, watching. How could He be so kind and loving to such foolish, careless sheep? They were always wandering off, still wanting their own way and ignoring His voice . . . yet, He kept right on loving them.

The night passed slowly and by early morning, the flock was restless and hungry. They wanted to move out and away from this place; but, The Shepherd held them back with one word—"Wait!"

Persnickety and Timidity were becoming quite perturbed at the long delay, and they let everyone know it.

"What are we waiting for?" Persnickety asked loudly.

"We could be miles away from here," muttered Timidity.

The impatient muttering spread slowly from one restless one to the other until . . . a slight shudder . . . beneath their feet . . . silenced them! Frozen with fear, they stood still.

Suddenly, the earth began to shake and rumble. Once again they fell to the ground, bumping and sliding into each other. Finally, as if exhausted, the shifting ground settled down into its stony stillness. Stunned, the sheep lay still also in the swirling dust.

Once again The Shepherd's voice rang out clear and strong:

"I'm here . . . don't be afraid."

At first the bewildered sheep were too numb with shock to move; they lay gasping for air. The Shepherd moved among them, speaking gently to each, calling them by name.

His presence and His voice were all they needed to quench the terror of the past wild moments and they were soon on their feet. Precious and Satisfied were speechless and trembling; but, their eyes were on The Shepherd's face and their ears were open to His voice. They moved close to His side, eager for those five special pats.

When The Shepherd shouted: "Follow Me!" new strength surged through the whole flock. The waiting was over . . . they were on their way!

"Yippee!" shouted Precious as he jumped around Satisfied, clicking his heels. She laughed, delighted by the rapid recovery of her friend.

"Aren't you glad we listened to Emmanuel and waited in the cleft of the rock, Precious?" she asked still smiling.

"He always knows best!" shouted Precious, still jumping . . . "Always and forever!"

Then, as if startled by the wonderful thought, he stopped in his tracks and added:

"All our lives He has provided whatever we needed and protected us from whatever would harm us . . . IF . . . if we did whatever He told us to do. Surely, we can trust Him whatever happens tomorrow!"

"Even an earthquake!" interrupted Satisfied.

"Yes! Even an earthquake," shouted Precious. "Surely His loving kindness and tender mercy will follow us all the days of our lives!

Thank You,

Thank You,

Thank You,

Thank You!"

Selah

pause and think about it

There is an unrelenting process going on all around and in us, at this very moment. It is either slow and silent or sudden and startling. It is the process of change and decay, growth and replenishment. We can ignore it, fight against it, argue with it . . . whatever; but, it continues.

In his book, More Than Meets The Eye, Richard Swenson takes us deeper into the meaning of a well-known verse of scripture:

"When Paul wrote, 'though outwardly we are wasting away; yet inwardly we are being renewed day by day,' apparently he was correct on both the spiritual and the physical levels.

The body contains between 10 and 100 trillion cells (and each cell contains approximately a trillion atoms). These cells, like just about everything else in the body, are continually being torn down, remodeled and replaced." 1

From the minute atoms to the majestic mountains, from the seasons to the styles—changing. Ah . . . but there is ONE who cannot be touched by change:

"For I am the Lord, I change not!" (Malachi 3:6–KJV)

"In the beginning You laid the foundations of the earth,
And the heavens are the work of Your hands.
They will all wear out like a garment.
Like clothing you will change them
And they will be discarded
But You remain the same.
And your years will never end." (Psalm 102:25-27–NIV)

In the first century, the Hebrew Christians began to waver in their faith; hard times began to dim the wonder of it all. The truth which they thought they cherished and understood was being ridiculed and challenged by the hostile, unbelieving crowd. They were becoming uncertain and afraid.

When the inspired writer declared to them that their Saviour, "Jesus Christ is the same yesterday and today and forever." Hebrews 13:18 (NIV), he was declaring that Jesus was God! What a declaration! No matter what they were going through, or what the future looked like—they could be sure that what Jesus said—He would do. He had ALL authority and power to keep His word!

For us this reassurance bursts out like the sun on a rainy day. In the storm of uncertainty—we can be SURE that God really means what He says! No wonder we press closer to the

Saviour as we grow older. We have had the opportunity to prove the faithfulness of God and finally realize that the things that gave us a feeling of security either change, disappoint, or fade away. We have discovered that He alone is our SURETY—our guarantee.

Shattering times will come; our world will be shaken. It may be just a shudder in a high wind . . . or an earthquake. Without warning, everything in our life can be shaken and all earthly security knocked out from under us.

Some years ago I watched my father slowly succumb to cancer of the lung. He was a tall, strong man, accustomed to hard work, with a great talent in repairing and building things. If something broke, I knew that dad could fix it—but, he couldn't fix this.

In his early years he had ignored the church and his relationship with God. But that changed as he grew older and he began to attend a little church down the street with my mother. When he retired he became custodian of the church. Although it was supposed to be part time, he spent most every day polishing, cleaning and fixing whatever was broken. He seemed to be saying, "I'm so sorry I neglected you all these years."

It was December in Chicago and the snow piled along the busy streets lay frozen under a black coat of exhaust from the traffic. The icy wind seemed to intensify the pain I felt in my heart. The winter was unrelenting and I longed for some kind of warmth and hope . . . like the Spring.

My mother and I took turns staying with Dad at the hospital and we were both very tired. I knew that she needed me there with her during this difficult time; but as Christmas drew near, I felt that I should go home for a few days to be with my husband and four children.

It was a relief to be back in my peaceful home in North Carolina—the sadness was out of sight for a while and I rested. But, two days later, we received a terrifying phone call . . . "Come quickly, your mother has had a heart attack—it looks bad."

I was stunned. She was not the one who was sick! "Oh, why did I leave her," I thought.

"She needed me and I left her, Lord, where are you?" We drove all night and arrived a few hours before she died. My world was shaking and I struggled to keep my balance. Half dazed, I walked into the hospital elevator that would take me to my father's room three floors above. I had to tell him the reason that she would not visit him that day.

On the afternoon of the funeral, we helped dad into his blue suit that had been hanging so long in his closet at home. Seeing him in that wheelchair, all dressed up, I found myself grasping for the hope that maybe he looked better. Maybe . . . if we drove home we would find mom busy in the kitchen, and I would discover that the pathos of the past weeks was only the drama of a very bad dream . . . but no. (The earth was shaking!) Dad was dying and we were on our way to mom's funeral.

We were walking in the valley and there was no turning back. I see now that we were following a flickering light there in the shadows. Emmanuel was there, not explaining, just silently guiding, strengthening, and urging us on; and He was giving me a longing to put some kind of beauty into the stark sadness.

This would be the last time on this side of eternity that I would see my father and mother in the same room. I wanted to say something personal, special to both of them. As a young girl I had loved to sing. Dad had never been present to hear me—this would be the last chance.

I don't know what that solo sounded like in those emotional moments; but I do know that if ever the heart could be heard singing it was then:

"My heart can sing when I pause to remember,
A heartache here is but a stepping stone -
Along a trail that's winding always upwards,
This troubled world is not my final home.

The things of earth will dim and lose their value,
If we recall they're borrowed for a while,
And things of earth that cause the heart to tremble,
Remembered there will only bring a smile.

This weary world with all it's toil and struggle,
May take its toll of misery and strife,
The soul of man is like a waiting falcon,
When its released its destined for the skies,
But,
Until then my heart will go on singing,
Until then with joy I'll carry on,
Until the day my eyes behold the city,
Until the day God calls me home." 2

Christmas Eve came. The little Christmas tree at the nurse's station glowed cheerfully in the midst of the quiet chaos in each room. Down the hall some children were singing Christmas carols. Dad opened the presents we brought to him and especially admired the plaid flannel shirt. He said he would be sure to wear that when he got home . . . we were all pretending.

Dad grew steadily weaker in the next few days. One morning as I walked toward his room, my aunt met me in the hall. She had stayed with him through the night, and I could see she was upset.

"He's been asking for you. He won't close his eyes," she said.

I sat down on the cot beside his bed. He looked so tired. I took his hand and looked into his eyes.

"What's wrong, daddy, why can't you close your eyes?"

"The devil's in there," he replied quickly. His words hit me like a blast of icy wind from outside. I wanted to say, "No, dad, you are probably dreaming." But in that instant, I realized that he was actually seeing a reality I could not see. The devil had been his prosecuting attorney for many years, and now, in his weakest moment, the enemy took off his disguise and showed himself—laughing and taunting him.

Unable to hide the quiver in my voice I said, "Maybe he is, dad, but because of what Jesus has done for you, you don't need to be scared of him any longer. This room is filled with angels. You don't have to be scared of him any longer; he's defeated, daddy!"

I was sitting as close to him as I could get, looking at him through the side-rails of that bed. He gazed intently into my eyes for a moment and asked softly . . . "Are you sure?" His desperate question nearly took my breath away. Standing there on the brink of eternity—this is what he wanted to know, and he had to know for sure—nothing else mattered. Every other need or desire was stripped away at that one eternal moment. I could feel the hidden spiritual battle going on in that room—that battleground. The devil and his army were gathered around, waiting for my answer . . . "Yes, daddy, I'm sure."

Trembling in sorrow, weak, yes . . . BUT SURE! That "mustard seed" cry of faith must have been big enough to clear that room, because dad closed his eyes and went into a deep, peaceful sleep. In fact, he slept so well that day that I decided to go home for the night instead of staying at the hospital.

Early the next morning, before I arrived—he died. The last words I heard him speak were, "Are you sure?" What a question! Thirty-three years have passed since that soul shaking moment and I am more sure than ever.

God has given us His word on it! I can be sure that He paid the debt for my sin:

"SURELY He took up our infirmities
and carried our sorrows
Yet we considered Him stricken by God,
Smitten of Him, and afflicted
BUT—He was pierced for our iniquities;
The punishment that brought us peace was upon Him,
And by His wound we are healed." (Isaiah 53: 4,5—NIV)

"He cancelled the record that contained the charges against us. He took it and destroyed it by nailing it to Christ's cross. In this way, GOD DISARMED THE EVIL RULERS AND AUTHORITIES. HE SHAMED THEM PUBLICLY BY HIS VICTORY OVER THEM ON THE CROSS OF CHRIST." (Colossians 2:14,15—NLT)

We don't have to be scared of him any longer—the devil has been defeated!

So that's the "SURELY" OF THE PAST—there is another one for these present moments . . .

"SURELY He will save you from the fowler's snare
and from the deadly pestilence He will cover you with His feathers,
and under His wings you will find refuge;
His faithfulness will be your shield and rampart." (Psalm 91:3,4—NIV)

If we pay attention, our Shepherd will point out the traps that the enemy has set for us, and we can avoid them. But, if we become careless and we stumble and fall, even then He is faithful to pick us up, dust us off and cover us with His love.

No wonder the Psalmist cried out:

"You thrill me, Lord, with all you have done for me!
I sing for joy because of what You have done." (Psalm 92:4—NLT)

God's love is ALL INCLUSIVE! Not only does He gently lead all through our journey of life, promising never to leave us on our own, but He has provided a REAR GUARD. Even though we are a part of the Shepherd's flock, enjoying His presence and provision, old enemies from the past tag along, hoping for a chance to draw us away and spoil our peace. Fear, worry, memories of past failure always seek to intrude. But God has assigned two guardian Angels to follow us all the way home. And they are there FOR SURE:

"SURELY Goodness and Mercy shall follow me all the days of my life. . . ."

1. "More Than Meets The Eye", Richard A. Swenson, M.D, p. 20, NAU Press, Bringing Truth to Life, P.O. Box 35001, Colorado Springs, Colorado 80935

2. "Until Then", Song by Stuart Hamblen, Hamblen Music Company, P.O. Box 46043, Hollywood, California 90046

He hath borne our griefs
and carried our sorrows.
Isaiah 53:4

He shall deliver thee
from the snare of the
fowler, and the noisome
pestilence. He shall cover
thee with His feathers
and under His wings
shalt thou trust.
Psalm 91:4

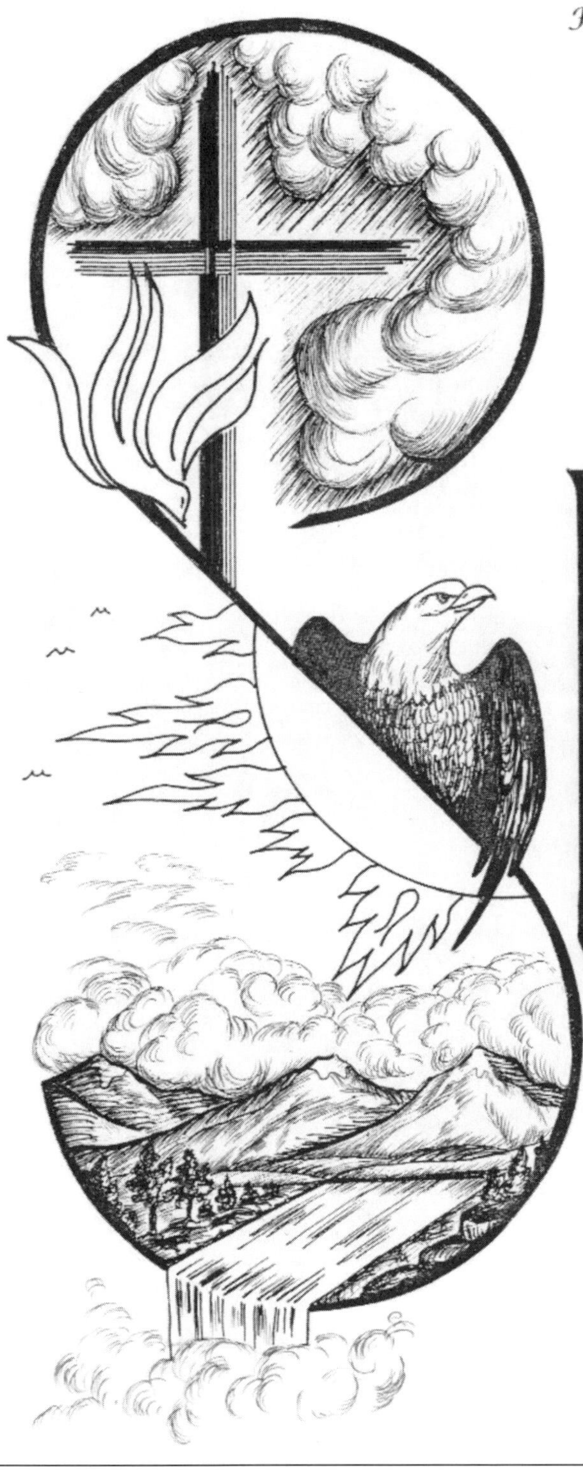

URELY

Goodness and
Mercy shall follow
me all the days
of my life
I shall dwell
in the House of
The Lord
Forever.
Psalm 23:6

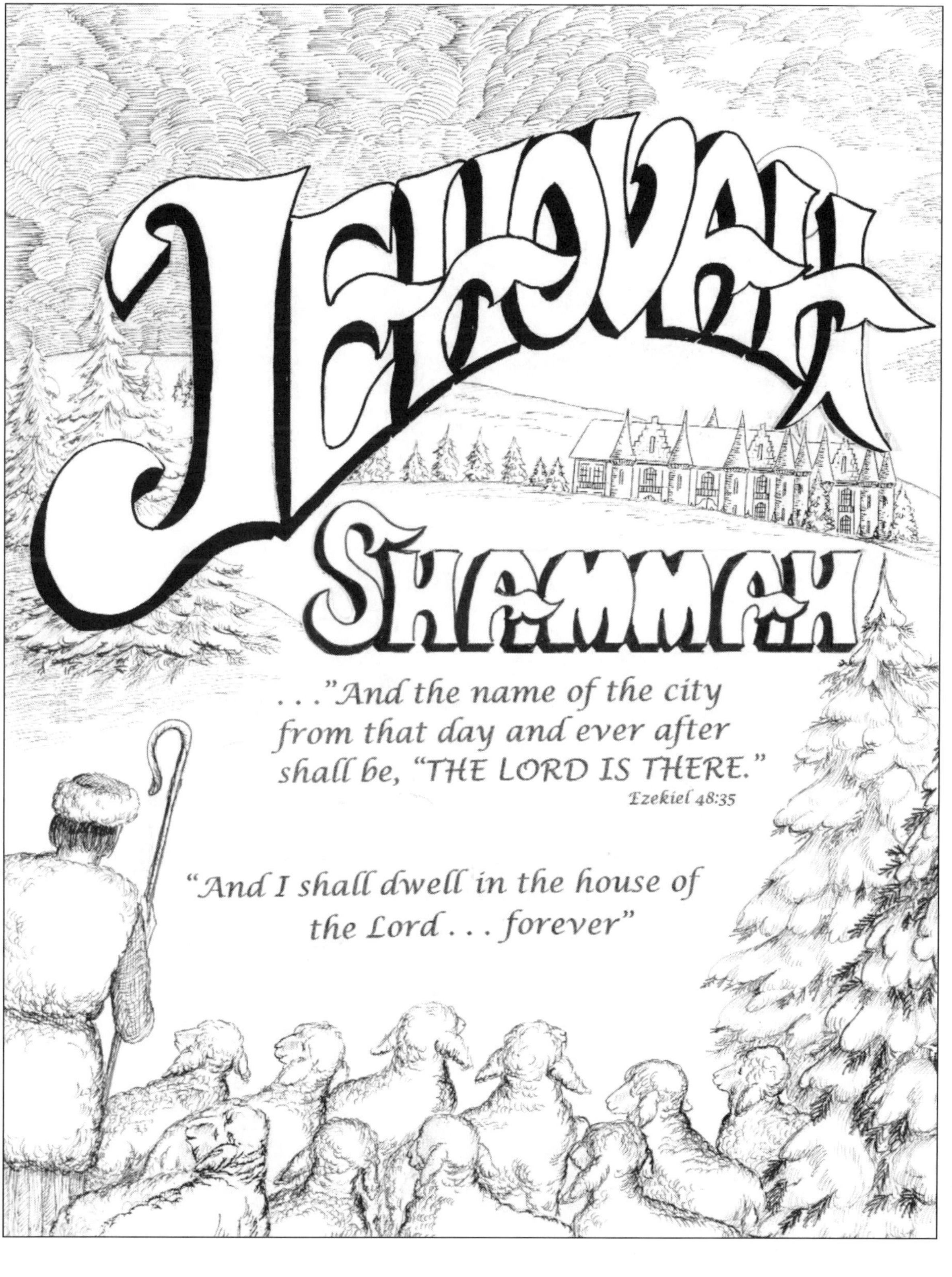
JEHOVAH
SHAMMAH
. . ."And the name of the city from that day and ever after shall be, "THE LORD IS THERE."
Ezekiel 48:35
"And I shall dwell in the house of the Lord . . . forever"

Chapter 10

Willy, Stubby, and Luke were not feeling well, to be sure, but they were ready to go. They limped obediently behind The Shepherd without a word of complaint. In fact, not one word of complaint could be heard from the whole flock. They were gratefully on their way and they were not looking back.

Reminders of the terrible shaking were all around them. They shuddered as they stepped over the muddy roots of the toppled trees that lay across their path. As The Shepherd carefully guided them around a deep fissure in the ground, bright sunrays pierced through the clouds as if eager to heal the brooding earth's gaping wounds.

Suddenly, the dark crevice sparkled and flashed. As the rays hit the crystals cracked open and released from their rock prisons. A rainbow of colors burst forth from the cleft as more of the crystalline minerals were exposed to the light of the sun!

This unexpected display of released radiance appeared so silently that most of the flock hardly noticed. But Precious and Satisfied stopped, captivated by the beautiful scintillation coming from the hole in the ground!

"How can all that beauty come out of such a deep, dark, and broken place?" Satisfied asked, looking quite bewildered.

"The sunlight found it," Precious replied quickly.

They both looked up when they heard Psalm's voice behind them.

"Beauty can come from brokenness if you look for it," she said, "But you are right, it's the light that finds it." Then she added quickly, "Come now lambs, we can get so fascinated by the sparkle that we take our eyes off The Shepherd! Come—we are on our way home! And she began to sing:

"I waited patiently for the Lord;
He turned to me and heard my cry.
He lifted me out of the slimy pit,
Out of the mud and mire;
He set my feet on a rock
And gave me a firm place to stand!"
(Psalm 40:1,2—NIV)

"Yippee!" they shouted as they began to run after The Shepherd. "He has given us a firm place to stand." In a few moments they were at The Shepherd's side, eager to see what lay on the other side of the mountain.

The icy wind, the downward slope and their ardent anticipation helped the flock move more rapidly that day. Although unmentioned through the past seasons of their lives, each sheep had a secret longing for a permanent place of provision.

Now, one special word was passing from one to the other as they descended the mountain. In this cold and lonely place, the wind seemed to whisper a warm promise and soothing hope of something good ahead . . . an end to their wandering . . . "home."

By late afternoon, cold weariness began to numb their eagerness. Although they longed to stop and rest, they knew by past experience that The Shepherd was aware of their needs, so they pressed on.

Finally, just as the sun began to unfold its curtain of red and gold, they limped out upon a fertile plateau. To their delight, supper was spread out before them. By the time the drapery of the day had closed, they were nestled together, sheltered from the wind in the refuge of the rocks. Warmed and satisfied, the weary sheep rested for the night.

High over their sleepy heads the icy wind began to blow the clouds aside and a great silver moon appeared and sparkled the frosty ground around them.

At the first hint of dawn, the flock was wide awake and ready to go. Precious and Satisfied were at The Shepherd's side when they reached the rim of the plateau. They gasped in surprise as they looked down, for stretched out into the distance, beyond the coastal plain, lay a great shining, silver-blue expanse—the Sea!

At first they gazed at the beautiful sight in wonder, but that wonder soon changed to gasping fear. They had crossed many streams and even a wide river, but how could they face this? Then remembering who stood beside them, they both looked up into Emmanuel's face, almost expecting a look of surprised concern—but they saw none. The Shepherd smiled at their upturned faces, for He knew them well.

He reached down and patted their puzzled heads (those five special pats), and said confidently: "Don't worry . . . I'm here."

That was all they needed to hear for He had never failed them in the past, and He always kept His Word!

Precious began to sing:

"Oh, when I am afraid
I will trust in You,
Oh, when I am afraid
I will trust in You,
Oh, when I am afraid
I will trust in You,
So now I can be very brave!"
(Taken from Psalm 56:3—NIV)

Even though it was a simple song, it contained profound trust. It was a song that the other sheep needed to hear at that tremulous moment. It planted a melody in their hearts and they hummed the tune all that day as they cautiously moved on to the coastal plain.

The land sloped gradually downward so they were able to travel more quickly. The sun was hidden by the gray, wintry clouds each day, and darkness came too quickly. It was a windy plain in any season, but now it seemed to greet them with a frigid fury from the sea.

Yet, in those chilling circumstances that might have made them faint and fall, they sensed a steady and sustaining strength that kept them going . . . the sight of The Shepherd walking confidently ahead encouraged them and the thought of home in the distance warmed them . . . so they went quietly on.

A tremor of excitement rippled through the whole flock when they reached the shoreline. They were stunned by the awesome immensity that stretched out before them!

Many times in past seasons, The Shepherd had led them beside STILL waters—but THIS was different! Great billows rose and curled and plunged—splashing their foam upon the strand. In a thousand voices, side by side, over and over, they leaped toward the land shouting in a thunderous whisper:

Ever-LASTING! . . . LASTING . . . LASTING . . . LASTING

Ever-LASTING! . . . LASTING . . . LASTING . . . LASTING

Ever-LASTING! . . . LASTING . . . LASTING . . . LASTING

On and on with relentless rhythm the waves surged in without intermission, as though determined to explain the meaning of the WIDENESS.

As Precious gazed at the vast expanse and listened, his emotions seemed to vacillate from astonished admiration to turbulent terror!

"Can't see the end, can you, lad?"

Precious was so deeply wrapped in his mixed emotions that he was startled by the calm voice of his old friend, Steady, who walked up beside him.

But in those few short words, Precious seemed to identify the problem. . . . It was the limitless extent and infinite vastness that overwhelmed him—he could not see the END!

Without one word of response to Steady, Precious ran to The Shepherd's side. The lamb had finally learned that He alone had the answers to his questions and the remedy for his confusion! Long ago he had given his future, with all its puzzlements, to The Shepherd, and now he just wanted to look into His face—that was all he needed.

To his great relief, The Shepherd did not look a bit worried or nervous. He stood calmly in the midst of His flock, enjoying the grandeur of the sea He knew so well. Precious thought to himself: "Well, if there is an end, Emmanuel has been there."

He chuckled as the stalker scampered off, stumbling as he ran!

Each day as they walked beside the ocean, the flock grew less timid. They began to realize that there was an unmarked boundary past which the waves would not go. They were growing accustomed to the awesome sight and sound of its depth and wideness.

But, early one morning, The Shepherd began to lead them inland. Feathery white flurries of snow drifted and swirled gently around their heads. Soon they had left the surf behind and were enfolded in a cool stillness. A soft, untouched carpet of white stretched out before them.

The way was beautiful . . . but it was cold and new. They all walked slowly with heads bent low. Suddenly, The Shepherd stopped and they all looked up.

There . . . not far ahead, golden lights glowed warm and bright. The Shepherd turned and looked down at His weary flock, shivering in the snow and shouted, with laughter in His voice ". . . Home Ahead!"

Joyful anticipation surged through the flock as they approached the entrance of Emmanuel's land. A high, white, shining gate swung open easily at the touch of His hand. As they entered, a most amazing change came over the whole flock. From the oldest ewe to the youngest lamb . . . all weariness and frowns disappeared as they eagerly pressed forward.

Precious and Satisfied were right at The Shepherd's heels so they were first in line, jumping about and shouting for joy. The Shepherd threw His head back and laughed at their revived energy as they entered in.

Psalm's face was shining and she was singing at the top of her voice:

"Enter into His gates with thanksgiving,
And into His courts with praise;
Be thankful unto Him,
And bless His name.

For The Lord is good
His mercy is everlasting;
And His truth endureth . . .
To all generations!"
(Psalm 100:4,5–KJV)

Persnickety and Timidity were laughing and trying their best to learn the words to her song. Cautious and Prudent were hugging each other and dancing. Willy, Luke, and Stubby, who had been near the end of the line, were pushing their way through the crowd, giggling and tripping over each other as they ran.

With eager, excited faces the sheep moved forward through the gate. Steadfast and Unity stood at the side, grinning from ear to ear, guiding them and making sure each one arrived safely . . . but eager to get inside themselves!

To their amazement, once inside the gate, it seemed they left the winter behind! Emmanuel's land was wonderfully shielded from the icy wind that had caused them such suffering. A gentle breeze whispered a welcome in their ears and a sweet fragrance from the myriad flowers along the path warmed their cold noses.

There, before their eyes, stretched a shining river, clear as crystal, coursing through the land. Tall fruit trees with glistening, green leaves stood like stately sentinels along the banks, nourished by the beautiful river.

NEVER . . . NEVER had they seen, or even imagined, a place so wondrously beautiful! In all the seasons of their lives . . . through all the meadows and mountains of their journey . . . nothing could be compared to this! With each new breath they seemed to feel stronger, for the air was fresh with joy. They could not hold back their laughter, for it was in the atmosphere!

Overwhelmed by the wonder of it all, Precious and Satisfied looked out over a vast meadow of green grass, so vivid in color that they seemed to be able to feel the color. Like waves of the sea, each silken blade swayed in perfect rhythm, responding to the music in the wind. Without question, they both recognized the song in the air. Each blade of grass and flower petal, free from blight or strangling weed, was singing a song of Praise to The Shepherd!

Suddenly, they realized that a great crowd, a flock of sheep far too many to count, was approaching. Although they were a great distance away the two could see each one very clearly. They were coming to welcome them! Right in front came "Faithful," who had left them in the Spring. Her wool was white and shiny, free from all briars or twigs, and her face glistened with radiant joy! Precious laughed as he remembered he had wished that she had never gone away! Oh, if only he would have known where she was, he never would have been sad at all–just as Emmanuel had said.

Satisfied whispered softly, "If I would have known what Emmanuel's land was like, I would have paid more attention to every word He spoke. If I would have known, I never would have complained about anything—anywhere. All the storms and heat, the gnats and flies—the rocks and mud, the pain and suffering all wrapped together could not be compared to one sight of this wondrous place!"

Together they turned and faced The Shepherd. He stood nearby watching, smiling in satisfaction, thoroughly delighted with their joy. With a hint of laughter in His voice, He said, "This is only the beginning! There is more . . . so much more! In my Father's house are many mansions—all prepared for you!"

Stunned with the reality of His great love, Satisfied began to cry. She looked into the face of her best friend, Precious, and saw big tears in his eyes, too.

"How could He be so kind to such unworthy ones?" whispered Precious. He said, "All our lives He has anticipated our needs before we even knew we had them . . . It's almost as though He was one with us . . . almost as though . . . He had the heart . . . of a LAMB!"

Now . . . they were not the only ones weeping. No one in the flock could hold back their tears of overpowering gratitude.

It was a magnificent moment . . . on that beautiful side of The Gate, as The Shepherd moved slowly from sheep to sheep, tenderly lifting each shaggy little head and wiping the tears from their eyes.

In the ecstasy of that wonderful moment, only two beautiful words could be heard . . .

thank you . . .

thank you . . .

thank you . . .

thank you . . .

thank you . . . as the flock with radiant faces . . . very precious and completely satisfied . . . followed Emmanuel into His Father's House.

Selah

pause and think about it

We give little thought to winter during the long sunny days of summer. Chilly winds and icy streets seem far away when the air is fragrant with the perfume from the flowers planted in the spring.

But, when the first frost surprises us one autumn morning, we begin to consider the inevitable approach of winter.

As a child we dream of what we will be "when we grow up." In this, our springtime, we are sprouting and growing as we head toward the summer of adulthood. In the long busy hours, our hands are occupied with building, tending and defending—and it seems as if these days are here to stay.

But, the season is changing, almost imperceptively—we can feel it in our bones. Harvest time arrives and our crop is coming in . . . we begin to reap what we have sown.

If we have ignored the direction and provision of the Great Gardener, Jesus, the autumn of our life is hard to bear. We cry out: "Oh, I didn't mean to become this."

No wonder we call this "the fall." It is the season when the leaves fall from the trees and what is underneath the greenery is revealed. All the bark ruined by insects, all the twisted, broken branches are in full view.

Youth is gone and no frantic attempt to stop the aging process works. What we have done to ourselves shows. Vitamins may help a bit, facials and face-lifts may offer a bit of hope in front of the mirror . . . but "the beat goes on."

So it can be a very sad, melancholy time for us when our life has been marred and broken with sin, when our hopes and dreams lay shattered at our feet.

Oh—but there is HOPE! Jesus is the great Restorer. He specializes in mending broken things! Centuries ago God spoke to a prophet named Jeremiah. The nation of Israel was ruined by rebellion and disobedience. It was a tragic time. In the midst of the gloom, God told Jeremiah that He had a message for him to give to the fallen nation. The prophet did not realize that message would be for us in the twenty-first century.

> *"Go down to the shop where clay pots are made," He said. "I will speak to you while you are there." So I did as He told me and found the potter working at his wheel. But the jar he was making did not turn out as he had hoped, so the potter squashed the jar into a lump of clay and started again.*
>
> *Then the Lord gave me this message; "O Israel, can I not do to you as this potter has done to his clay? As the clay is in the potter's hand so are you in my hand." (Jeremiah 18:2-6—NLT)*

There was some impurity in that lump of clay that kept it from yielding to the potter's creative hand; perhaps it fell apart.

Jeremiah must have expected the potter to toss it aside; there was plenty of clay at his disposal. Why waste time on this lump? But to the prophet's surprise, the potter picked up the pieces and began to work with that same lump of clay . . . and he made it again—into something useful, even beautiful!

This is a portrait of Sovereign Grace—God's goodness and mercy in action.

"He heals the brokenhearted and binds up their wounds (curing their pains and their sorrows)." (Psalm 147:3—Amplified Bible)

Jesus said that this was the reason God had sent Him into this world of broken things.

"The Spirit of the Lord is upon me, because He hath anointed me to preach the gospel to the poor. He has sent me to HEAL THE BROKEN-HEARTED, to preach deliverance to the captives, and recovering of sight to the blind, to set at liberty them that are bruised." (Luke 4:18—KJV)

Here is the unfathomable mystery of the ages! He was anointed to preach to the poor . . . He became poor, born in a stable.

He was sent to heal the broken-hearted . . . His heart was broken as He wept over Jerusalem.

He was sent to preach deliverance to the captives . . . He became the captive—arrested in the garden, dragged before Pilot.

He was sent to set at liberty them that are bruised . . . He was bruised and beaten and spat upon for our iniquity!

What condescension! The Great Shepherd laid aside His splendor and came down, down, down, from heaven's glory to earth's gory . . . THE SHEPHERD BECAME THE LAMB, the perfect, spotless, sinless sacrifice.

So, saved by the Blood of The Lamb and led by the hand of The Shepherd, we contemplate eternity.

In our early years, thoughts of the end of life here are rare, we feel so permanent. But when our hair is "touched with the light of Emmanuel's hand" (as someone in the past has said), we become aware of our frailty and the accelerated passing of time.

We all walk beside the Sea of Eternity. Beautiful, or frightening as it may be, it is a sight we have never seen before and its overwhelming dimension leaves us breathless. Death marks the end of time as we know it. Just as the sea is awesome because we can't see the end of it, even so with Eternity . . . there is NO END. In our present measurement of life, everything has an end somewhere.

How utterly foolish it is to spend a lifetime concentrating on a tiny segment that is ending, splashing in a little pond that is drying up—with no consideration or preparation for the wide Sea of Eternity straight ahead.

Our Dearest of All has crossed the uncharted expanse and cleared the way for us to follow—not into the dark unknown, but a place prepared . . . Home. It is beautiful beyond words, peaceful beyond comprehension, wonderful beyond imagining, beyond . . . beyond . . . beyond:

"No eye has seen, nor ear has heard,
and no mind has imagined
what God has prepared
for those who love him!"
(1 Corinthians 2:9–NLT)

No . . . we can't imagine, but we do know that the atmosphere of heaven is permeated with JOY:

"You will show me the path of life: IN YOUR PRESENCE IS FULLNESS OF JOY, at your right hand there are pleasures forevermore." (Psalm 16:11–Amplified Bible)

Not just joy—but FULLNESS of joy . . . abundant, overflowing, complete and everlasting! This joy is the marvelous result of what is NOT there . . . the list is long!

Hunger

Thirst

Sickness

Hurt Feelings

Broken Promises

Fear

Sorrow

Pain

Tears

Enemies

Separation

Night

Evil

. . . just to mention a few.

No wonder there is JOY . . . all hindrances gone, all waiting ended, all hopes satisfied, all promises fulfilled—forever in His presence!

Is it not remarkable that something so wonderful, this JOY, would be available to us now, while we walk this planet? When Jesus left heaven's glory and appeared in that little dusty stable in Bethlehem, He brought the joy of heaven with Him. After that, He gave it to each one who touched Him as Saviour.

But, it doesn't stop there. When we share the jubilance of our salvation with someone else, that JOY is sent back to heaven:

> *"I say unto you, that likewise joy shall be in heaven over one sinner that repenteth more than ninety and nine just persons which need no repentance." (Luke 15:7—KJV)*

The joy that we experience here is only a "bud," but it continues to grow even during the drought and stormy winds of this life. One bright day, at the end of our seasons—it bursts into full bloom in the presence of God.

I believe that I caught a glimpse of Glory—a hint of that joy in the midst of great sadness. My father died a few days after my mother's sudden death and the strain had left me emotionally drained. My father lay in the funeral home now. I came into the quiet room to be alone with him one last time before all the family and friends arrived.

Suddenly the thin wall of my self-control crumbled and I began to sob hysterically, I cried out to the Lord:

"Lord, you seem so far way—this is so hard to bear. Dad was the one who was sick, and mom died! Now he's gone . . . prayer didn't seem to matter. I know I'm wrong . . . but it looks like You have failed me. I know I'm wrong. I know I'm wrong . . . help me to see what is going on here!"

It was not a feeble cry of abandoned faith, but of tested faith—faith under fire. Because in that instant the sobbing stopped; I couldn't cry. Instead, I found myself smiling as though I was suddenly in the middle of something wonderful.

I was aware of my father standing beside me on the right, smiling. He said with a hint of laughter in his voice:

"You know those things we were talking about? . . . they're true!"

In those days in the hospital he had memorized Psalm 23 down to "Yea, though I walk through the valley of the shadow of death, I will fear no evil, for Thou art with me.." We had talked about heaven and what it must be like. He had said, "That's nice, but I want to stay here for a while." It was all different now. Now he said: "Erwin's here"—and my big brother who had died ten years before this, leaned forward from dad's right side and said, smiling: "Hi, Esther."

My mother was standing beside me on my left. Her face was beaming, and in that beautiful German accent that I knew so well, she said:

"Don't vorry about those tings!"(Don't worry about those things!)

I knew exactly what she meant. All her "things" at home were just as she had left them. They had been so important to her once . . . her new watch on the dresser, her slippers by the bed, her clothes in the closet, her coffee cup in the sink. I didn't want anything disturbed . . . they were hers.

But now she had gleefully discarded them all—they did not matter, and I needed to understand that. There were times when I had seen my parents enjoying a bit of happiness. But it seems that all happiness "has strings attached." We know that it won't last, for we have no idea what is around the corner. In a moment, the ring of the telephone, a knock at the door, a cruel word, a change of mood—and it is gone. Happiness is a very fragile thing, hard to hang on to.

This was something different than an expression of frail happiness. It was a peaceful confidence . . . a display of the finished product. Everything had been explained . . . all corrections made, all pain relieved, all fears forgotten. They had finished writing the last page of the last chapter of their book . . . the ropes that had bound them to the earth were snapped and they WERE FREE from worry about anything or anybody . . . FREE JOY!

Months later, I found an old picture of my mother that came close to it. She was twenty-three years old, on board a ship sailing from a hard life in Germany to America, "the land of plenty." Seated on deck, with the wind blowing her hair, the wide expanse of ocean behind her—she was smiling, absolutely thrilled in anticipation of a wonderful new life in America!

In that funeral home, the somber atmosphere of that room, so accustomed to tears, was changed. Now I stood surrounded by peaceful, triumphant, "everything under control," exaltation! I felt that if I turned around I would see a great crowd of people watching me . . . a huge crowd of witnesses to the life of faith.

But then, like a vapor, it was all gone—my aunt entered the room. I tried to describe what had just happened and she smiled sympathetically and patted me on the shoulder.

In the weeks that followed, things began to settle down to normal back in my home in North Carolina. But, I could not forget that experience in the funeral home. I went over and over each detail. Finally, one day I came to the conclusion that it had to have been my imagination (WHAT AN IMAGINATION!). If it would have been "real," Erwin would have been standing next to my mother. She had grieved for him for years.

But, then I remembered that ten years before this I stood in the same funeral home after my brother had died. My dad was with me in the room and I said to him, "Dad, if you don't receive Jesus as your Saviour—you will never see Erwin again." Dad had said to me . . . "Erwin's here!"

As the months passed, a beautiful truth emerged out of the shadows . . . THINGS ARE NOT WHAT THEY SEEM TO BE! What looks like a tragedy, for a child of God, one who belongs to the Good Shepherd, one who knows Emmanuel, the DEAREST of all—IT IS A TRIUMPH!

In my opinion whatever we may have to go through now is less than nothing compared with the magnificent future God has planned for us. The whole creation is on tiptoe to see the wonderful sight of the sons of God coming into their own. The world of creation CANNOT AS YET SEE REALITY, not because it chooses to be blind, but because in God's purpose it has been so limited—yet it has been given hope. And the hope is that in the end the whole of created life will be rescued from the tyranny of change and decay and have its share in the magnificent LIBERTY which can only belong to the children of God!"
(Romans 8:18-20—J. B. Phillips)

> *"These little troubles (which are really so transitory) are winning for us a permanent, glorious and solid reward out of all proportion to our pain. FOR WE ARE LOOKING ALL THE TIME NOT AT THE VISIBLE THINGS BUT AT THE INVISIBLE. THE VISIBLE THINGS ARE TRANSITORY: IT IS THE INVISIBLE THINGS THAT ARE REALLY PERMANENT." (2 Corinthians 4:17,18–J. B. Phillips)*

". . . AND I WILL DWELL IN THE HOUSE OF THE LORD FOREVER!" Oh, to hear our Father say:

> *"Well done, thou good and faithful servant; thou hast been faithful over a few things, I will make thee ruler over many things: ENTER THOU INTO THE JOY OF THY LORD!" (Matthew 25:21–KJV)*

And we will say . . . Thank You! Thank You!

Thank You,

Thank You,

Thank You,

Thank You,

Thank You,

Thank You!

Thank You!

Oh, Thank You!

The Shepherd King

The Shepherd's staff
He carefully cut and fashioned from the tree,
Fits well His hand
That safely led His flock along the way;
Through quiet streams,
Through shadowed glens and fearful mountain heights.
Each wandering one
Would feel its touch that swept them back in line.

But now....
Fall down in awe
And wonder as the Shepherd takes the throne!
Almighty God!
He smashes nations with an iron rod....
The Conqueror
Of warring souls, defeating death and hell.
Crown Him! Crown Him!
The Shepherd holds a scepter in His hand!